WOMEN, TAKE YOUR PLACE

Susan Pryor

Women, Take Your Place
By Susan Pryor

ISBN: 978-0-578-62728-1

Copyright © 2019 Susan Pryor

Interior design: Aydin Tasdeler
Cover design: Aydin Tasdeler
Editor: Megan Tasdeler

Published by: Psalm 45 Publishing

To God who calls us out
To Jesus who journeys with us
To Holy Spirit who lights our way

All scriptures are quoted from the New American Standard Bible unless otherwise noted.

To all handmaidens of God,
past, present, and future –

May we rise in His glory and serve in His honor.

TABLE OF CONTENTS

INTRODUCTION

God is mightily manifesting His presence in these beginning days of yet another great and holy outpouring of His Spirit. He can and does sovereignly move to draw men and women unto Him and to change their hearts toward Him with mighty acts that amaze and wonders that astonish. However, He also chooses to move through the ministry of those cleansed by the power of His blood, the saints in His Church. He asks them to be the ministering agents of His grace, mercy, love, and power on earth. While His kingdom in heaven has no problem with this plan, His Church on earth definitely has.

A core area in which the Church struggles centers around the role of women. Has anyone noticed the disparity between the number of men who serve God in areas of responsibility in His Church and the number of women who do so? Has anyone asked why the proportion of men in ministry is so much higher than that of women in ministry? Has anyone questioned whether the norm of male domination in the Church was established through biblical instruction or through human tradition? Are any curious as to how some of the ungodly views and statements of Greek and Roman philosophers and early Church fathers have caused women to be in spiritual bondage for centuries? Has anyone checked whether the work of Bible translators is accurate or if personal and cultural prejudice against women has produced erroneous renderings and inaccurate interpretations of the Bible?

We are now aware that God is on the move. Jesus said that He would build His Church (Matthew 16:18). Is His Church a gender-biased, women-disparaging body? Is His Church patterned after the laws and the all-male hierarchy of authority and power of the Old Testament temple? Is His Church based on denominations which are under the thrall of unholy traditions declaring that men should rule and occupy all church offices and that forbid women from leadership positions? Does His Church allow the male half of the body to pursue its callings, while the female half is locked into a few, minor roles?

When God moves in might, He expects His people to move with Him. That is not possible if fifty percent of the saints are forbidden from having a part in what He is doing. When His Spirit moves in power, He desires that His Church be the expression of His will. That is not possible if half of His workforce is effectively laid off.

Through the pages of this book, may we take a new look at the women in God's Church? May we ascertain if what we have been taught about their positions and appointments in His Church is true or false? May we determine God's will and plan for His women based on His Word? And, after all this is done, may women finally be allowed to take their rightful place in His kingdom?

Chapter 1

THE SOURCES OF ERROR

"Beware lest anyone cheat you through philosophy and empty deceit, according to the tradition of men, according to the basic principles of the world, and not according to Christ." (Colossians 2:8 NKJV)

Just as unholy "isms," moral aberrations, and rebellion against God's marriage covenant have caused widespread problems with God's created order, so also mankind's historical abuse of women, its determined efforts to subjugate them, and its refusal to allow them to walk in their God-ordained roles in life are causing havoc in society. Sadly, this last perversion is as widespread in the Church as it is in the world.

There have been widespread sin with and abuse of the first command given by God to mankind: *"Be fruitful and multiply"* (Genesis 1:28). So also, there have been worldwide, sweeping, pervasive errors concerning the second command to *"have dominion...."* (Genesis 1:28).

From the earliest days of humanity's presence on earth unto the present hour, people have ignorantly or deliberately misunderstood, misinterpreted, and mistaken God's will for women. Hence, they have been the consistent impediment for women taking their rightful place and fulfilling His will. While many factors have played a role in this aberration, in the Church two major areas have caused foundational problems concerning the issue of the place of women: Greek influence on society and translational error. Both can be seen in the difficult-to-understand passages in the epistles of Paul, a first century apostle whose words about women have often been distorted.

GREEK INFLUENCE

Long ago, some Greeks who studied the "wisdom of men," such as Socrates and Aristotle, began to promote their erroneous ideas of the inferiority of women. So influential were their thoughts and so quoted were their words that their philosophies eventually became the way of life in Greek and Roman cultures. When Paul wrote his letters, his words, rather than addressing this error, were misinterpreted to conform to the thoughts of pagan philosophers. Further, first-century Greek converts to Christianity brought their Greek ideas into the embryonic Christian community and influenced that body with their bias against and disdain for women. This influence lead to the teaching that God cursed all women through Eve's sin. The biblical scholar Jerome suffered from these wrong beliefs and distain towards women, particularly pregnant women.[1] He then incorporated this bias into the Latin Vulgate translation of the Bible around 382 AD. Unfortunately, since the Vulgate was by far the most commonly used Bible until the Reformation over a thousand years later, Jerome's prejudices have had a huge impact on Western civilization's views on women.

ERRORS IN TRANSLATION

Many native English speakers believe that what words mean in English is exactly what they mean in other languages. Sometimes that is true, but other times it is

[1] Barr, Jane. "The Vulgate Genesis and St. Jerome's Attitude To Women," *saylor.org,* n.d., https://resources.saylor.org/wwwresources/archived/site/wp-content/uploads/2011/04/The-Vulgate-Genesis.pdf. Accessed 9 Sep 2019.

decidedly not. Much of the Bible was originally written in Greek, and many believe that the original Greek exactly translates into English or that the meanings of various Greek words exactly correspond to English words. Yet, this is not always the case. Sometimes, the English language is deficient and may not provide the variety of meanings, shades, or nuances found in a Greek word.

For example, in English, we have one word for praise. However, in the original Greek, many words for praise exist, each of which conveys different aspects of it, commands different expressions of it, or describes different forms of it. One such word is *halal*,[2] which occurs often in Psalms 113-118. It means to shine, to boast, to make a show, to rave, to celebrate, and to be clamorously foolish. Another word for praise is *yadah*,[3] which is used in Psalm 42:5. *Yadah* means to use (i.e. to hold out) the hand, to revere, or to worship with extended hands. It is used when honoring God for His mercies, works, and goodness, whether past, present, or future. While both *halal* and *yadah* mean praise, each indicates a specific type of praise.

Such problems of translation are particularly prevalent in Paul's epistles. The words he chose when writing his letters to the newborn Church to establish doctrinal authority contain shades of meaning not obvious in English. Therefore, they were not conveyed when his words were translated into English. It might then be a surprise to learn that Paul did not write some of the things that the Church and the world have been taught he wrote. In fact:

- Paul didn't believe in the inferiority of women. Instead,

[2] "Greek/Hebrew Definitions," *Bible Tools,* Bibletools.org, n.d., https://www.bibletools.org/index.cfm/fuseaction/Lexicon.show/ID/H1984/halal.htm. Accessed 8 Aug 2019.

[3] "Greek/Hebrew Definitions," *Bible Tools*, BibleTools.org, n.d., https://www.bibletools.org/index.cfm/fuseaction/Lexicon.show/ID/h3034/page/2. Accessed 8 Aug 2019.

he was an unabashed advocate of their spiritual equality with men.

- Paul didn't promote the idea of male superiority. Instead, he championed the value of women.

- Paul didn't establish a hierarchy of control over women. Instead, he gave women authority.

- Paul didn't require women to have a secondary role in the Church. Instead, he honored them with up-front ministry.

- Paul didn't see women as second-class citizens or believe that the female half of God's creation was inferior. Instead, he saw them as learned leaders who had the right to exercise authority under authority just as Christ had taught.

How odd and sad it is that instead of setting precedence and communicating a clear message of gender affirmation and equality, the words of Paul have become the primary vehicle of the depreciation and oppression of women, especially in the Church. The final section of this book looks at this distorted message in order to set the record straight.

To ensure that God's Word is the final arbiter of truth, in this last section of this book, a more teaching style of writing will be used. Questionable words will be set apart, their numbers and their basic meanings as listed in *Strong's Exhaustive Concordance Of The Bible*[4] will be noted in the hope that the Bereans (Acts 17:11) among us, those who check Scripture for accuracy, will become the sons of Issachar (1 Chronicles 12:32), those who see and know the signs of the times and know what ought to be done.

---

[4] Strong, James. *The New Strong's Exhaustive Concordance Of The Bible*, Thomas Nelson, Publisher, 1984.

Chapter 2

GENESIS 1 – "HE" OR "THEY"?

*"God blessed **them**, and God said to **them**...."* [emphasis added] (Genesis 1:28)

In the book of Genesis verses are found which have been grievously misunderstood and erroneously quoted. Errors springing from their faulty translation have misrepresented both the identity and function of women. These verses have been and are still used to promote the theories that, in identity, women are inferior to men and that, in function, women should not be allowed to exercise godly authority or to serve God in positions equal to or over those of men. Since God's Word stands true, a short explanation of these difficult passages should bring freedom to the women – and the men – who are in bondage concerning them.

In the beginning, God created. For six days, He created everything that was created.

- Day 1: He created light (Genesis 1:3-5).
- Day 2: He created the heavens (Genesis 1:6-8).
- Day 3: He created the earth and seas, the grass, herbs, seeds, and trees (Genesis 1:9-12).
- Day 4: He created the sun, moon, and stars (Genesis 1:14-18).
- Day 5: He created the sea creatures and the birds (Genesis 1:20-22).

- Day 6: He created the animals to inhabit the earth (Genesis 1:24-25).

God also had some interesting comments about His handiwork. In every case except one, on every day except the day He created the heavens, God created and saw that it was good. Then came the zenith or climax of His labors. He created mankind.

> Then God said, "Let Us make man in Our mage, according to Our likeness; and let them rule over the fish of the sea and over the birds of the sky and over the cattle and over all the earth, and over every creeping thing that creeps on the earth." God created man in His own image; in the image of God He created him; male and female He created them. (Genesis 1:26-27)

Several things should stand out here. First, God created two distinct, separate sexes, one male and one female. Second, mankind alone has the honor of being created in the image of God; none of the rest of creation has this distinction. Third, in creating mankind, God combined two worlds – the material and immaterial or the worlds of flesh and of spirit. Finally, these verses should explode the myth that females were created inferior to males in either identity or function.

CONCERNING IDENTITY: FEMALES WERE NOT CREATED INFERIOR TO MALES

According to Genesis 1:27, God created mankind in His image and likeness. According to *Strong's Exhaustive Concordance Of The Bible,* the word translated as man is *adham* (120), and it refers to mankind, usually in the collective sense. It can also refer to a creature in God's image or the crown of creation. Finally, it can refer to a specific man, such as Adam himself. Yet, the overall context of Genesis 1:27 strongly implies that this verse is not referring just to Adam but to all mankind.

In creating mankind God created two separate genders, male and female, in His likeness. *Strong's* shows that the word for male is *zakar* (2145), and it means maleness, as opposed to femaleness, or the male sex or gender. Also, the word for female is *neqeba* (5347), which means woman, not a man, or opposite of man.

Some people claim that since God created Adam first, Eve was created inferior to Adam. Thus, since she is the first and representative female, all females are inferior to males. However, this view is incorrect. Being created after Adam does not make Eve inferior to Adam any more than Adam being created after fish, birds, and animals makes him inferior to them. Another erroneous belief is that since Eve was taken out of Adam's side, she was inferior to him. However, the truth is that being taken from Adam's side does not make Eve inferior to him any more than taking Adam from the ground makes him inferior to the ground. A third inaccurate idea comes from the facts that God molded man out of the dirt from ground and that He blew the breath of life into him (Genesis 2:7), but that He drew woman out of man (Genesis 2:21-22). Some conclude from this that God created Adam in his own image, but then He created woman in the image of man. However, Genesis 1:26-28 makes it clear that God created both male and female in the image of God.

Since no part of God can be inferior, neither gender created in His image could have been inferior. Therefore, those who claim that females were created as an inferior gender are in some way saying that God was inferior when He was not.

While male and female were created perfectly in His likeness, they were not created as clones. Some notable differences existed between them. They were created different biologically, with males tending to have more height, hair, and muscles, and to have deeper voices than women. The two sexes also had different sexual organs. They were not unisex, or having the sexes blended or obliterated until both became one neutral gender. Nor were they androgynous, or having the characteristics of both sexes. They were simply male and female.

That there were differences created in them mentally is also evident. As can be seen even today, in areas of ideas, concepts, preconceptions, logic, reasoning, and emotions, men and women think about, perceive, and feel about the same things differently. Men tend to work on one task at a time, while women can multitask. Men tend to keep the main point in mind while women remember details. Men are less talkative than women. Men are more competitive while women are more sociable. Men crave respect while women crave love.

Yet, spiritually, they were created equal. Spiritually, neither was inferior to the other since they were both created in the image of perfect God.

CONCERNING FUNCTION: MALE AND FEMALE WERE TO OCCUPY AN EXALTED POSITION OVER THE REST OF CREATION

> God blessed **them**, and God said to **them**, "Be fruitful and multiply, and fill the earth, and subdue it; and rule over the fish of the sea and over the birds of the sky and over every living thing that moves on the earth." [emphasis added] (Genesis 1:28)

Note the use of the word them in this passage. God gave both of them, the male and the female, the mandate to be fruitful and multiply. He also gave both of them the command to rule. It would require joint stewardship to fully accomplish these tasks. Just as God never intended man to multiply by himself by making it physically impossible for him to do so, so He never intended him to exercise dominion over creation by himself. In partnership, shared responsibility, and mutual respect, man and woman together were to increase and together were to exercise dominion in obedience to God. *Strong's Exhaustive Concordance of the Bible* informs us about the word for dominion, *radah* (7287). *Radah* means to tread down, to subjugate, to subdue, to rule, to prevail against, or to reign over.

Due to their oneness, the man and the woman were given the same order. Due to their differences, they had separate means to accomplish or fulfill this task. Neither was superior or inferior to the other.

As both were created like God, both were given His authority to act as His stewards or surrogates. As both Adam and Eve were co-equal in identity, so they were co-equal in function.

Contrary to the teachings of the ages, woman was not created a slave, an underling, a gopher, or a flunky. She was comparable to man and given the same mandates.

Nowhere in these verses concerning God's creation is it stated that man was intended to rule over woman. Thus far in His directive, God has indicated two areas of authority: His over mankind and mankind's over creation. He gave no degree, command, or implication that man was to tread down, subjugate, subdue, rule over, prevail against, or reign over woman. It just does not exist in creation Scripture.

Only God was in authority over mankind. Neither male nor female was given the right to usurp authority over the other. Neither was given the right to rule over the other. It was not part of God's intent. His intent was partnership and co-rule, not subjugation.

When God was done creating mankind, when He had

created male and female in His image with the blessing of joint authority, *"God saw all that He had made, and behold, it was very good"* (Genesis 1:31).

THE TRUTH

While God made men and women different physically and mentally, He made them equal spiritually, for both were created in the image of God. As their Creator, God has authority over them, and while He has given them joint authority over the rest of creation, He did not give either of them authority over the other.

Chapter 3

GENESIS 2 – GOD'S COMMAND TO MANKIND

"The LORD God commanded the man, saying…."
(Genesis 2:16)

After God created man and breathed life into him, He placed him in a garden called Eden. In the middle of this lovely spot were the tree of life and the tree of the knowledge of good and evil. It was God's intent that man should keep and tend this garden.

Then things began to get interesting:

*The LORD God **commanded the man,** saying, "From every tree of the garden you may eat freely; but from the tree of the knowledge of good and evil you shall not eat, for in the day that you eat from it you will surely die."* [emphasis added] (Genesis 2:16-17)

The words of this decree are written in the second person singular. Since woman had not yet been created, the word man is a specific reference to Adam. Note well that before woman existed, God spoke to Adam and gave him, not them, the order about the trees. His words were a blessing, a command, and a warning.

Then God continued His plan: *"Then the LORD God said, 'It is not good for the man to be alone; I will make him a helper suitable for him'"* (Genesis 2:18).

When commenting on creation earlier (Genesis 1:31), the LORD God looked and declared His work to be good. In Genesis 2:18, something is not good. Specifically, it was not good for man to be alone. According to *Strong's Exhaustive Concordance of the Bible*, the word alone is *bad* (905), and it means to have separation, like part of a body or the branch of a tree; to be apart or by self; or to be solitary. It was not good that the man was separated.

Therefore, the question must be answered, separated from whom or from what? Did God mean that Adam was separated from God? Absolutely not! God had created Adam as a spiritual being who walked and talked with him in perfect communion. He intended that man should always be in touch with Him.

Was Adam separated from the rest of creation? In one sense, yes! Man had been created differently and higher than the rest of creation. Not an object in space or a plant or animal on the earth, Adam was to maintain an identity apart from the lower orders of creation. Yet, in another sense, no! Man had to remain in relationship with the rest of creation to rule over it.

Was Adam separated from a mate? Yes! The other animals were not alone. Each had a match or a mate. But not man. Therefore, God saw it was not good that Adam did not have a mate or a wife. In the eyes of God, a void, a deficiency, or an incompletion existed that was caused by man's singleness. Since man was alone, God moved. He created a helper who would be comparable with him.

> *So the LORD God caused a deep sleep to fall on the man, and he slept; then He took one of his ribs and closed up the flesh at that place. The LORD God fashioned into a woman the rib which He had taken from the man and brought her to the man. (Genesis*

2:21-22)

Three things are worthy of note here. First, it was God who created man's companion. His idea, His power, and His creativity brought forth woman to His own satisfaction. Dare any challenge His decisions?

Second, the word for help or helper is *ezer* (5825). *Strong's Exhaustive Concordance of the Bible* shows that *ezer* means to surround, protect, and succor. It does not mean servant or slave or subservient one. It does not indicate a bullied, subjugated workhorse. It means a partner, an assistant, an aide, or a co-worker.

That the word used for helper does not indicate subservience is further indicated by the fact that it is used seven times in the Old Testament to refer to God Himself, who is subservient to no one. For example, Psalm 121:2 says, *"My help [ezer] comes from the LORD, who made heaven and earth."* No one thinks that help from the LORD is inferior or that the LORD who is offering help is to be treated as a slave or as a lowly or menial creature. Therefore, these meanings should not be attributed in reference to women either. Though created to be a helper or a companion or a co-worker, woman was not created to be a slave or an underling.

Third, the woman was to be comparable to man. *Strong's Concordance* tells us that the word for comparable is *nehghed* (5048), and it means part, opposite, counterpart, or mate. The idea was for her to be separate from but a completion of the man. Though two individuals are involved, they are yet one whole. They stand alongside each other and yet blend with each other to manifest, help, and praise the other.

When God brought woman to Adam, he accepted her. His words are familiar: *"This is now bone of my bones, and flesh of my flesh; she shall be called Woman, because she was taken from Man"* (Genesis 2:23). *Strong's Exhaustive Concordance of the Bible* states that the word from is *nagad* (5046), which means to stand boldly opposite; to manifest; to expose, explain, or predict; or to praise. When God exposed Eve to Adam, she stood boldly opposite him and he praised her. Further, *Strong's* shows that the word for woman is *ishshah* (802), which is wife or bride. So, the woman who came from the man was to be his wife.

God's will from the beginning was to take man, who was alone, and from him bring forth woman so that the one became two. Yet, it was also His will that man should be joined to woman and that the two should become one flesh (Genesis 2:24).

THE TRUTH

God saw it was not good for man to be alone, and He created woman as the answer to the problem. She was a partner, the completion of man. She was not his downtrodden servant.

Chapter 4

GENESIS 3 – THE FALL

"Now the serpent was more crafty than any beast of the field which the LORD God had made. And he said to the woman, 'Indeed, has God said, "You shall not eat from any tree of the garden"?'" (Genesis 3:1)

Genesis 3 is an astonishing chapter in the Bible. If read carefully, it exposes truth about the events in the garden of Eden. Its revelations fall into several sections: the fall, the accounting, the verdict, and the aftermath.

THE FALL

How the serpent got into the garden and how he knew what God had or had not said to Adam and Eve is not recorded in Scripture. Nevertheless, the purpose of his attack is obvious: he wanted to introduce doubt and confusion. His question to Eve was designed to find out what she knew and where her weakness was so he would know exactly how to lead her into evil. Further, he wanted to make God appear to be less than loving and kind. His unholy implication that God had limited her enjoyment of the garden by placing restrictions on a supposedly particularly desirable fruit made Him seem mean spirited. Finally, the serpent used the occasion to introduce unholy cravings. He wanted to make Adam and Eve focus on desires of the flesh and yearn for that which was forbidden.

To gain his end, the serpent approached Eve in the garden and spoke to her. His oily, treacherous question seemed innocent enough. *"Indeed, has God said, 'You shall not eat from any tree of the garden'?"* (Genesis 3:1).

The woman's mistake was in responding to the serpent instead of immediately taking the situation to God. At least when she did answer the serpent, she began by defending God and speaking the truth. *"The woman said to the serpent, 'From the fruit of the trees of the garden we may eat'"* (Genesis 3:2).

Sadly, she then fell into error. She both added to and misquoted the command from God. *"[B]ut from the fruit of the tree which is in the middle of the garden, God has said, 'You shall not eat from it or touch it, or you will die'"* (Genesis 3:3).

In two areas, the woman was mistaken. The tree of life was in the center of the garden (Genesis 2:9) and mankind was not banned from eating its fruit and being infused with its life. Further, God had never said not to touch the fruit of the tree for fear of death.

Now the serpent stopped beating around the bush. After successfully engaging the woman in conversation and clouding her judgment, he dropped all attempt at subtlety. Using deception as a weapon, he attacked.

> *The serpent said to the woman, "You surely will not die! For God knows that in the day you eat from it your eyes will be opened, and you will be like God, knowing good and evil." When the woman saw that the tree was good for food, and that it was a delight to the eyes, and that the tree was desirable to make one wise, she took from its fruit and ate; and she gave also to her husband with her, and he ate.* (Genesis 3:4-6)

So, she fell.

And the man fell.

THE ACCOUNTING

As bad as that was, things got worse. God, who knew exactly what had happened, came to demand an accounting. First, He approached Adam to ask for his explanation. *"Then the LORD God called to the man, and said to him, 'Where are you?' ... And He said, ... 'Have you eaten from the tree of which I commanded you not to eat?'"* (Genesis 3:9-11).

Then Adam failed his test. Rather than acknowledge his own guilt, he initially blamed Eve for his behavior. *"The woman ... she gave me from the tree, and I ate"* (Genesis 3:12). Walking even deeper into sin, he also dared to blame God. *"The woman whom You gave to be with me...."* (Genesis 3:12). Adam's finger pointing indicated that he refused all responsibility for the tragedy.

Next, God asked the woman for her version. *"Then the LORD God said to the woman, 'What is this you have done?' And the woman said, 'The serpent deceived me, and I ate'"* (Genesis 3:13).

This was neither a repeat of Adam's denial nor an attempt to say, "the devil made me do it." This was straightforward accountability. She did not excuse herself; she accused herself. She did not point her finger at anyone else; she pointed it at herself. She did not blame others; she blamed herself. Seen in this light, her words stating that she recognized that the serpent had deceived her, that she had fallen into temptation, and that she had done exactly what God had said not to do are a confession of her sin to God.

THE VERDICT

Finally, God approached the serpent. Pointedly

enough, He did not ask him what had happened, for He knew what had happened. He simply declared the serpent guilty and cursed him.

> *"Because you have done this, cursed are you more than all cattle, and more than every beast of the field; on your belly you will go, and dust you will eat all the days of your life; and I will put enmity between you and the woman, and between your seed and her Seed; He shall bruise you on the head, and you shall bruise Him on the heel."* (Genesis 3:14-15).

Then, in reverse order of His demand for accounting, God gave His verdicts. To the woman, He said, *"I will greatly multiply your sorrow and your conception; in pain you shall bring forth children; your desire shall be for your husband, and he shall rule over you"* (Genesis 3:16 NKJV).

By His words, God declared three things. His words seem clear and easily understandable, but are the commonly accepted translations of these words an accurate depiction of His intent?

First, Genesis 3:16a seems to have been translated in a straightforward way: women were to know pain and sorrow, specifically in the area of childbearing. There is no doubt that throughout the course of human history, women have borne children in pain. Yet, in the Septuagint[5] version of the Bible, an alternative translation of this same phrase breaks with the traditional wording and introduces a whole new thought. Instead of the accepted translation of Genesis 3:16a, Katharine Bushnell states[6] that this verse may be

[5] The word Septuagint means seventy. Seventy-two scholars met in Alexandria, Egypt about 285 BC and translated the Old Testament writings from Hebrew to Greek. This version of Scripture was considered as close to the original Hebrew meaning as any had been up to that point. It was the version from which Jesus often quoted.

[6] Bushnell, Katharine. *God's Word To Women,* God's Word To Women, 2005, p. 51.

more accurately rendered as, *"A snare has increased your sorrow and sighing."*

These words vastly change the meaning of the verse. Instead of eternally condemning Eve and her female descendants to a lifetime of pain for an unforgivable sin, the focus is on what the enemy, not the woman, had done. The serpent's snare, his bait or trap for her, had indeed brought guilt, shame, and sorrow upon her.

Next, the words of Genesis 3:16b, which are translated as *"Your desire shall be for your husband,"* seem to indicate a change of relationship between the woman and her husband. *Strong's Concordance* states that the word for husband is *ish* (376), which means a male marriage partner.

Again, problems with the translation have arisen. For instance, *Strong's Concordance* informs us that desire is the Greek word *teshuqa* (8669), which means yearning, longing, or stretching out after. The traditional understanding of this word incorporates the idea of lust or sexual desire. In other words, it has been used to teach generations of married couples that the heart, mind, thoughts, and sexual desire of every wife should be toward her husband.

However, that meaning is biblically questionable. *Teshuqa* really means to long after, to stretch out after, or a turning from or to. Since these two meanings, sexual desire or a turning from, are not the same in content or intent, the use of this word in other passages of the Bible are the true indication of its meaning here. The word *teshuqa* is found three times in the Old Testament: Genesis 3:16; Genesis 4:7, and Song of Solomon 7:10.

Genesis 4:7 says, *"If you do well, will you not be accepted? And if you do not do well, sin lies at the door. And its desire is for you, but you should rule over it."* In its context, these words can in no way be misunderstood as a discussion of sexual yearning. Speaking to Cain, God is declaring that sin is at his door, that it desired him, and that he should master or turn away from it.

Song of Solomon 7:10 reads, *"I am my beloved's, and his desire is toward me."* Here the Shulamite is declaring that she belongs to her beloved and that he is turning toward her. The idea is affection and longing, not sensuality.

In neither of these verses is the predominating thought of lust. Therefore, it cannot imply or be accurately translated to mean sexual desire in the passage in Genesis 3:16b either. A more correct translation of this verse would be, *"You are turning away from me to your husband."*

Finally, in Genesis 3:16c, there is a problem with the meaning of the words *"shall rule."* The commonly quoted words, *"he shall rule over you"* seem to indicate a change in life's order. *Strong's* shows that the word for rule is *mashal* (4910), which is to govern, to have dominion, to manage, or to appropriate leadership over. Thus, these words have been understood to be a mandate for male supremacy and as permission for the male to assume total authority over the female. Such mishandling of the truth has led to error, chaos, and tragedy.

However, like the errors of Genesis 3:16a and 3:16b, the problem with the word shall stems from poor translation. In this case, shall does not appear in the original versions and was later inserted by translators. If, as many believe, the word shall should really be will, then this verse is not in the imperative. That is, it is not a command that men must do. Rather, it was prophetic of what they might do.

God was giving a prophetic declaration, not a holy decree. Instead of putting a curse on the woman or pronouncing a punishment, He was, in fact, issuing a warning. Combining the earlier meanings of these verses, Genesis 3:16b,c should read: "You are in danger of turning away from me toward your husband – of preferring him over

Me. And if you do, there will be consequences. You will bring yourself under his dominion or rule."

One important thing to realize is that when God had finished speaking to Eve, He did not mention a curse. Though it is so often assumed and taught that He did, **God did not curse the woman.** In these passages of Scripture, those words do not exist. In fact, because the woman made a good choice by openly revealing the source of her temptation, confessing her sin, and breaking with Satan, God honored her.

How did He do so? First, God created an enmity between the serpent and the woman (Genesis 3:15). That enmity led to a separation in their relationship. It announced that the woman was neither in league with nor an associate of the evil one.

Further, God declared that the enmity would not just bless the woman only but would extend His grace and mercy to her descendants too. In a future generation, the warfare would be so intense that though the serpent would bruise the heel of one of her descendants, that One, the Seed, would bruise the serpent's head. That holy Seed was the Messiah. This promise could not be made with someone in union with another who was eternally under a curse. God would not allow such a wonderful event as the birth of the Savior of the world to transpire through a cursed woman. Thus, He did not curse the woman; instead, in His love and mercy, He blessed her.

Then God spoke to Adam.

"Because you have heeded the voice of your wife, and have eaten from the tree of which I commanded you, saying, 'You shall not eat of it': cursed is the ground for your sake; in toil you shall eat of it all the days of your life. Both thorns and thistles it shall bring forth for you, and you shall eat of the herb of the field.

In the sweat of your face you shall eat bread.'" (Genesis 3:17-19)

Since Adam had listened to another voice and had followed a command contrary to the one given to him by God, his life was to be one of labor. He was no longer to tend the garden but to toil in life.

Due to his choice to sin, the ground was now cursed. The changes in it caused thorns and thistles to grow in what had once been pristine glory. Those things once there to sustain life easily now had to be worked for. The man would toil for its fruits until the day he died. However, though God cursed the ground, He did not curse Adam.

Notice the differences leading up to the verdicts against man and woman.

1. After Eve sinned, she admitted her guilt. Yet, after Adam sinned, he did not. Though both were guilty, the woman is the only one who confessed sin.

2. Both the woman and the man chose to eat of the fruit. They both made their own decision to do what God had said they must not do. Eve did not make Adam do anything; she could not make Adam do anything. She chose; he chose.

3. The woman was deceived, but Adam sinned with his eyes wide open (1 Timothy 2:14). The woman was tricked by the serpent. *Strong's Concordance* tells us that the word used here for deceived, *apateo* (538), means beguiled, duped, tricked, or deceived wholly. It means thoroughly, completely, without any doubt deceived. She really did not know. Adam, though, was well aware of the magnitude of the sin and did it anyway.

THE AFTERMATH

First, sin entered the world through the man's actions. God gave the man the command not to eat of the fruit of the tree of the knowledge of good and evil (Genesis 2:17). He did not give this command to the woman because she had not yet been created. Therefore, God challenged the man, but not the woman, about his actions: *"Have you eaten from the tree of which I commanded you not to eat?"* (Genesis 3:11). In addition, Adam had been present in the garden when the woman was tempted and had done nothing to correct or stop her, as seen in Genesis 3:6: *"she gave also to her husband with her, and he ate."* Due to this, God placed the blame for the sin squarely on the man. In His eyes, it was through man, not woman, that sin entered the world. *"Therefore, just as through one man sin entered into the world...."* (Romans 5:12).

Second, death entered the world. As forewarned in Genesis 2:17, Adam, and every subsequent human being, would eventually die physically. *"[T]ill you return to the ground, because from it you were taken; for you are dust, and to dust you shall return"* (Genesis 3:19).

Third, for the first time, Adam called the woman Eve. Throughout the passage of time from the creation of man and woman to their fall and judgment, the woman had no name. Now, the man, Adam, named the woman Eve. *"Now the man called his wife's name Eve, because she was the mother of all the living"* (Genesis 3:20).

The significance of this is great. When someone names something, it is an indication that it is under the stewardship or the care of the one who names it. For example, when a person names an animal it is an indication of his or her ownership of and responsibility for that creature. Similarly, when someone names a business, it indicates he or she owns and is responsible for the proper running of that entity. Just so, after the judgment Adam named Eve, which suggested a change in the marital relationship. It was an indication that he was in some way to be a proprietary caretaker or benevolent keeper. However, this change nowhere suggests that she was to lose her identity or her mandate to rule in partnership with her husband.

Too, a name is a discernment of the person. It often describes an attribute or character trait or speaks prophetically of the person. According to *Strong's Exhaustive Concordance of the Bible*, the word for Eve is *chavvah* (2332), and it means to live or to be a life giver. Eve was indeed the mother of all living. By so naming her, Adam was acknowledging the truth: while he was the father of sin and death, she was mother of the living.

Fourth, the man was cast out of the garden.

Then the LORD God said, "Behold, the man has become like one of Us, knowing good and evil; and now, he might stretch out his hand, and take also from the tree of life, and eat, and live forever." Therefore, the LORD God sent him out from the garden of Eden, to cultivate the ground from which he was taken. (Genesis 3:22-23)

In these verses, by His use of the masculine, singular pronoun, God was speaking of Adam only. He did not say that they (Adam and Eve) had a problem but that he (Adam) did. Specifically, because Adam had become like God and because Adam might eat of the tree of life, he was sent out of the garden.

Contrary to common belief, God did not eject both Adam and Eve from the garden. His order was for Adam to leave, and he did so. Perhaps, as God had warned, Eve chose her relationship with Adam over her relationship with God, because, as Genesis 4:1 reveals, at some point, she left the garden and was again united with Adam.

Fifth, the long-term consequence of sin was death. Not only would Adam die, but, through him, death would enter the human race.

For as in Adam, all die.... (1 Corinthians 15:22)

Therefore, just as through one man sin entered into the world, and death through sin, and so death spread to all men.... (Romans 5:12)

Before ending this chapter, one point is well worth reiterating. God did not curse either the man or the woman. Yes, Eve's sin was judged and punished, but she was not cursed. Likewise, though Adam's sin was judged and punished, he was not cursed.

In fact, in His mercy, *"The LORD God made garments of skin for Adam and his wife and clothed them"* (Genesis 3:21). God slew innocent animals and used their skins to cover the couple. This was a type or shadow of the future system of animal sacrifice to atone for or cover the sins of men and women and of the death of the innocent Lamb of God whose blood was shed for the forgiveness of the sins of all mankind.

Since Eve was forgiven rather than cursed, no curse came through her line onto all her female descendants. God's Word is clear that man, not woman, brought sin and death to the human race. So, why is it that woman, not man, has historically, culturally, and religiously been blamed for the debacle in the garden? Unfortunately, that which God prophesied might happen has indeed come to pass: women have come under the rule of men.

THE TRUTH

While both Adam and Eve sinned by eating of the forbidden fruit, only Eve acknowledged and confessed her sin to God. As a result of their disobedience, sin entered the once-perfect world and mankind began to suffer physical death. Adam was ordered to leave the garden, and Eve chose to go with him. Despite these facts, women are blamed for this debacle.

Chapter 5

THE GENTILES AND THE JEWS

*"But a woman who fears the LORD, she shall be praised.
Give her of the fruit of her hands, and let her own works
praise her in the gates."* (Proverbs 31:31)

Adam and Eve's fall changed history. Their judgment and punishment have affected all of mankind. Since much error, terror, and abuse can trace its source back to the first generation of mankind, the subject of the curse is worth closer study.

CURSES

In the Old Testament, the word curse is *arar (799)*. According to *Strong's Exhaustive Concordance of the Bible*, it was a pronouncement of judgment on anyone who broke covenant. Too, it was to lay anathema on someone or something. For example, Balak hired Balaam to curse the Israelites (Numbers 23:11). Under the Old Covenant, the land (Isaiah 24:6); a specific tribe of Israel, the Gibeonites (Joshua 9:23); a group of young boys (2 Kings 2:24); and the individuals Cain (Genesis 4:11) and Canaan (Genesis 9:25) were cursed. Further, in the aftermath of the fall, God cursed the serpent (Genesis 3:14) and the ground (Genesis 3:17). In later Hebrew history, a curse was specifically the result of disobedience to the Law (Deuteronomy 27:13-26).

As the events in Eden prove, curses came with

disobedience. However, under the Old Covenant, God could turn a curse into a blessing because of His great love (Deuteronomy 23:5). Note well, He did not curse Adam and Eve. Yes, they were judged and punished, but their sin was covered by God. Yes, they left the garden, but they had been forgiven, not cursed.

The fallacy that Eve brought sin into the human race, that she had then been cursed, that her curse brought the same curse on every female descendant, or that her guilt is the guilt of all women is completely disproved by the Bible.

The truth is that sin entered the world through the sin of man (Romans 5:12), and then it became an ingrained part of human nature. Mercifully, God blessed those in sin by not imputing their sin to them until the Law was given. *"[F]or until the Law sin was in the world, but sin is not imputed when there is no law"* (Romans 5:13). When God did institute the Law through Moses, men and women were subject to it, and when they violated it, sin was imputed to them. They were then required to offer appropriate sacrifices for their sins to be atoned for or covered.

The word curse or *katara* (2671) is also found in the New Testament. In *Strong's Concordance,* it indicates an imprecation uttered out of malevolence or declares a sentence of divine judgment and the ruin that comes as a result. This word is used in reference to the Law: *"For as many as are of the works of the Law are under a curse"* (Galatians 3:10). For those who believe, God removed the curse through His Son, Jesus Christ, because He became a curse for us (Galatians 3:13-14). Through His one perfect sacrifice, the forgiveness of all sin committed anywhere by anyone at any time was made available to everyone.

Eve's sin was taken care of long ago, because God forgave both Adam and Eve. He took care of the sins of women living both before and under the Old Covenant, and He has taken care of the sins of women who have asked

Him to do so through the blood of Jesus Christ under the New Covenant. Therefore, women today are not responsible for Eve's error and ought not to be judged as blameworthy because of her sin.

MISPLACED BLAME

In spite of the fact that the Old Testament testifies that Adam was irresponsible and a covenant transgressor (Job 31:33; Hosea 6:7) and that the New Testament declares that one man is responsible for sin, judgment, and death entering the world (Romans 5:12-19), the Word of God has not been heard. Instead, the word of man has been listened to. As a result, the woman is still blamed for the fall and its ramifications.

Since God had pronounced enmity between Eve and the serpent and her Seed and his (Genesis 3:15), it is obvious that the serpent began to focus his hostility toward her. Further, since she did indeed turn away from God to man, she came under the rule of man (Genesis 3:16). With the evil nature of the serpent, Satan, and the carnal nature of man battling against her, a system developed that began to deprive women of their rightful place in life – and in God. It set into motion that war that we know to this day as the battle of the sexes.

Man and woman were separated from God and became estranged or alienated from each other. A power struggle ensued. Completing each other became competing with each other. Helping each other became attempting to rule over one another. Harmony became disharmony.

The carnal nature that now ruled man led him into conflict, compulsion, abuse, and tyranny. His target? Women! In the ages and generations that followed the events in the Garden of Eden, God's prophecy that men would rule women exploded into male chauvinism, domination, and supremacy. Women became subject to every whim and cruelty of men.

The Greeks And Their Treatment Of Women

From the dawn of creation until the days of the dominance of Greek culture, the idea grew that women were physically, mentally, emotionally, morally, and spiritually inferior to men. In particular, it was believed that women's lack of intellect and morality led to evil in the world. Therefore, for their own good and for the good of society, they should be treated differently than men and should be protected from themselves.

In *God's Word To Women*, Katharine Bushnell suggests that the first accusations that a woman was the source of all evil came from pagan myth:[7]

According to Hesiod, who lived about 800BC, Jupiter was angry because Prometheus had stolen fire from heaven, and in revenge ordered Vulcan to make a beautiful woman. Minerva adorned her with all gifts but Mercury gave her a deceitful mind. Named Pandora, she was brought to Epimetheus, who received her, contrary to warnings, in the absence of Prometheus. When admitted among men, Pandora opened a casket and allowed to escape all the evils of mankind, excepting delusive hope.

As years passed, this myth took on a reality. The tale of Pandora, who supposedly loosed a cascade of evil on mankind, was linked and equated to the story of Eve in Genesis. Two or three hundred years before Jesus came, this erroneous belief had been written into Apocryphal literature and the teaching of the Talmud, giving this amalgamation of myth and lies a stamp of authority. It then laid a basis for the cultural and religious abuses against

[7] Bushnell, Katharine. *God's Word To Women*, God's Word To Women, 2005, p. 37.

women that sprang up in both Greek and Hebrew societies.

Athens was named for the Greek goddess Athena and was a center of learning, philosophy, and culture. "How ironic that a system of philosophy that maintains that in all ways females are inferior to males should originate in a city named after a female deity who embodied wisdom."[8]

Socrates was a well-known and prestigious philosopher who lived in Athens around 470 to 399 BC. His influential words of contempt for women have made a deep impression on mankind to this very day. He referred to them as the weaker sex, said that being born a woman was a divine punishment, and claimed that women were halfway between men and animals. While in many ways he advocated shared duties between men and women, his question remained: "Do you know anything at all practiced among mankind in which in all these respects the male sex is not far better than the female?"[9]

His pupil, Plato, had a slightly better view of women and believed they should be educated. However, he also believed they were inferior to men and that men who were cowardly and lazy would be reborn as women in their next lives.[10]

His pupil, Aristotle (384-322 BC), added cement to the foundation of sexual inequality laid by Socrates. Aristotle affirmed the ideas that males were superior to females and that males were the rulers and women were the subjects. He taught that man, who was like the soul, was meant to

---

[8] Bristow, John Temple. *What Paul REALLY Said About Women: The Apostle's Liberating Views on Equality in Marriage, Leadership, and Love,* Harper One, 1991, p. 3.

[9] ibid. p. 4.

[10] Plato. *Great Dialogues of Plato,* Translated by W.H.D. Rouse, Mentor, 1956, p. 456.

command the woman, who was like the body. Although he did recognize that a society cannot be happy if women are not happy, he also stated that women were "defective and misbegotten."[11]

In addition to philosophers trumpeting a spurious doctrine against women, other notable Greek men spoke against women. Demosthenes, a renowned orator said, "We have courtesans for our pleasures, prostitutes for daily physical use, wives to bring up legitimate children and to be faithful stewards in household matters."[12] Since these public men were (and still are) influential, their pronouncements indoctrinated Greek minds with the ideas that women were inferior, that they were to be commanded by men, and that they could be used for the pleasure of men.

The Reality Of Life For Greek Women

In ancient Greece (except for Sparta), women were treated as little better than slaves. Culturally, they were secluded at home, prevented from going out alone, and forbidden from interacting with men not from their own family. They could, however, visit female friends and participate in religious festivals. While women were expected to remain chaste and faithful to their husbands, husbands were not expected to do so in return. It was common for men to have mistresses and to hire prostitutes.

Socially, other than some clothes and jewelry, women could not own property. Women could only inherit if there were no male relatives remaining, and even then, the

[11] Marshall, Taylor. "Eve – Is Woman A Misbegotten Male? (Thomas Aquinas)," *New Saint Thomas Institute,* TaylorMarshall.com, 8 Jul 2014, https://taylormarshall.com/2014/07/video-woman-misbegotten-male.html. Accessed 1 Sep 2019.

[12] Bristow, John Temple. *What Paul REALLY Said About Women: The Apostle's Liberating Views on Equality in Marriage, Leadership, and Love,* Harper One, 1991, p. 7.

inheritance was given to their husbands. They had limited social and recreational activities and were excluded from sports, business, voting, and holding public office.

In poor families it was not uncommon for baby girls to be left out in the elements to die. Young girls did receive basic education in reading, writing, and mathematics but then often focused on more artistic skills like music and dance. Families of young teenage girls arranged marriages for them, and the girls were expected to be virgins when they married. Women were to run their households and to raise children.

Two types of women lived outside these restrictive norms. The first group were the priestesses who served in the temples of the goddesses. The second group consisted of the sex workers, and the high-end prostitutes and courtesans tended to be more well-educated and influential (for obvious reasons) than the average woman.

The Hebrews And Their Treatment Of Women

One would hope that with the availability of the written law, history, and prophets and with the arrival of the Septuagint around 284 BC that the attitude of the Jewish society toward women would differ considerably that that of the pagan world, but it did not.

Old Testament scriptures detailed several prominent women, some of whom had authority over men. Rahab risked all for the Lord (Joshua 2, 6); Deborah sent Barak into war against the Canaanites (Judges 4-5); Jael killed Sisera, a captain of the enemy army (Judges 4:17-22); Ruth's faithfulness led to her becoming the ancestor of King David (Ruth 1-4); Esther saved her people from genocide (Esther 1-9); Abigail acted contrary to her husband's foolish orders and was blessed for doing so by David and by God (1 Samuel 25), and Huldah the prophetess gave wise counsel to a delegation of priests and leaders sent to her by King Josiah (2 Kings 22:12-20). Further, Proverbs 31 speaks of the ideal woman, one who is to be highly honored and considered a gift from God.

Yet, in large part, especially in the four hundred years that preceded the coming of Christ, the rabbis came under the influence of the Greek ideas and cultural habits. They began to imitate them instead of working to change them.

Without question, the four hundred years before Jesus came were difficult ones for the Jews. Since God was silent, they could not hear from Him or be instructed by His voice. In those days, known as the "days of mingling," Jewish teaching synchronized with Greek philosophy and Jewish custom blended with Hellenic lifestyle.

The chosen ones were to be a separate people. Yet, instead of remaining strangers to the unlimited boundaries and dissipations of worldly cultures and customs, they began to follow foreign manners and worldviews. Adopting Greek customs, they too went to gymnasiums, theaters, and sporting events. Further, rather than remaining untainted by worldly mindsets and heathen ideologies, they began to accept and practice ungodly ideas.

Inevitably, during this time the adopted mindset of female inferiority and servitude learned from their Greek contemporaries led to a diminishing of the value of Jewish women. In increasing numbers, the rabbis scorned and despised women in their teachings and oral traditions. Even the reputable and learned historian, Josephus, felt contempt for women. In his words, "The wife is inferior to the husband in all things."[13]

This negative view of women, whose source was ungodly and outside of Scripture, took root. Instead of being

[13] Josephus, Flavius. *The Works of Flavius Josephus*, Translated by John E. Beardsley, 1895, p. 226.

changed by Scripture, this belief challenged and imposed itself on Scripture. The result was that custom and culture dictated the interpretation of Scripture rather than Scripture dictating custom and culture.

The Reality Of Life For Jewish Women

Compared to their Greek counterparts, first-century Jewish women found life a bit easier. However, their legal and social position was still quite low. A traditional morning prayer from the Talmud recited by Jewish men was, "Blessed are you, Lord, our God, ruler of the universe who has not created me a woman." Some Pharisees, who were prominent religious and political leaders, were known as the "bruised and bleeding ones" because they shut their eyes whenever they saw a woman on the streets, thus causing them to walk into walls.[14] The Essenes even left behind a Dead Sea Scroll about the "Wiles of the Wanton Woman," which reflected their fear of and contempt for women.[15]

Culturally, the male, whether father or husband, was the unchallenged head of the home. An unmarried woman was under the control of her father and a married woman was under the control of her husband. Marriages were arranged, and women were expected to be virgins on their wedding night. A husband could divorce his new wife if she was found not to be a virgin. In addition, since the word wife is included with houses, servants, and animals in the listing of a man's possessions or objects that were not to be

[14] Barclay, William. "William Barclay's Daily Study Bible: Matthew 23," *Bible Commentaries,* StudyLight.org, n.d., https://www.studylight.org/commentaries/dsb/matthew-23.html. Accessed 23 Aug 2019.

[15] Broshi, Magen. "Beware the Wiles of the Wanton Woman, Magen Broshi, Biblical Archeological Review, Jul-Aug 1983," *Center For Online Judaic Studies,* n.d., http://cojs.org/beware _the_wiles_of_the_wanton_woman-_magen_broshi-_biblical_ archaeology_review-_jul-aug_1983/. Accessed 28 Aug 2019.

coveted in Exodus 20:17, some men interpreted this as meaning that their wives were possessions, too.

Legally, women had few rights. They could not testify in a court of law, hold public office, or vote. They also could not inherit property unless it was overseen by a male guardian who was appointed to do so. In addition, no husband had to honor a business deal made by his wife.

Religiously, the basis of holy life was worship in the temple where males comprised the priesthood and where males performed all religious duties. Though women were not obligated to attend feasts and perform rituals as men were, they could do so. They also could attend synagogue services if they sat in a segregated spot behind a screen where they could not be seen.

Educationally, it was common belief that to instruct a woman was to cast pearls before swine. Women were trained in household tasks but were not educated beyond that. If a father chose to teach his daughter from the Torah, it had to be done quietly at home. A common saying about this was, "It is better to see the Torah burnt than to hear its words on the lips of a woman."[16] Further, if a women somehow did obtain knowledge about a subject, she was not allowed to teach it to others, even to young children.

Socially, a woman was relegated to the home. Although she was allowed to leave it, she did not so do often. When she did go out in public, she had to adhere to cultural restrictions. It was improper for a woman to speak to a man in public; if she did so, her husband could divorce her as it was assumed that she was having an adulterous relationship with the man to whom she spoke. If adultery could be proven, by a curious double standard, though women were often stoned for this sin, men seldom were.

[16] Bristow, John Temple. *What Paul REALLY Said About Women: The Apostle's Liberating Views on Equality in Marriage, Leadership, and Love,* Harper One, 1991, p. 20.

THE TRUTH

The Bible is clear that God forgave both Adam and Eve of their sin in the garden of Eden and that it is through Adam that sin entered the world. Despite this, over the years an insidious and erroneous belief grew in Greek and Hebrew societies which declared women were inferior to men in every way. Thus, they were made subject to men and treated shamefully.

> *Now there were some Greeks among those who were going up to worship at the feast; these then came to Philip, who was from Bethsaida of Galilee, and began to ask him, saying, "Sir, we wish to see Jesus."* (John 12:20-22)

Oh, that all Greeks and the myriads of men and women who have been affected by their biased, prejudicial preaching that were birthed from pagan philosophy and myth would also ask to see Jesus, so He could reveal how far their hearts have been from holy truth.

Chapter 6

JESUS AND WOMEN

"Woman, believe Me, your hour is coming…." (John 4:21)

When Jesus arrived on the scene, the time was ripe for the cultural wars between Greeks and Jews and the social wars between male and female to end. Though the Gentile way should have been overcome by the Jewish way in the strength of their Scripture and their God, the Jews had become like the Gentiles instead. Now, both were being asked to become like Christ.

Jesus burst into this scene of cultural, ethnic, social, and religious male chauvinism. His words and His example challenged human traditions. Jesus gave women value. He showed them kindness and care. He lifted them out of obscurity and degradation, treated them fairly, and taught them. He spoke to women publicly, made disciples of them, healed them, delivered them, and raised them from the dead.

When Jesus came, religion was a male bastion from which women were totally excluded. In a radical, world-changing way and as a reflection of the Father's heart, Jesus advocated the inclusion of women in every aspect of ministry. The Savior of souls, the Advocate of rights, and the Deliverer of those held captive had come to challenge tradition and custom, prejudice and fear. He had come to change men's minds toward women.

Understand that this was a culture war of the greatest magnitude. It pitted the established Greek and Jewish social and religious customs against God. It challenged and declared wrong hundreds of years of error and tradition and of evil, exploitation, and abuse. It also provided a working model of right.

Jesus came to establish a new communion that modeled God's plan of creation. He came to eliminate the misinterpretations of the Old Testament and the abuses of human tradition and to establish a Church that would be a haven of harmony, peace, and cooperation between the sexes as had been intended from the beginning.

Jesus was clear that His earthly ministry was for women as well as men. He included women in His communal miracles (Matthew 14:13-21), healed them (Matthew 8:14-15; 9:20-22), delivered them (Matthew 15:21-28), and raised them from the dead (Matthew 9:24-25).

Further, Jesus' actions broke long-standing but erroneous social traditions. For example, Lazarus's sister, Mary, sat at Jesus' feet, the position of a student with a teacher (Luke 10:38-42), blowing away the prejudice against educating women. When scribes and Pharisees brought a woman to Jesus and hypocritically accused her but not her partner of adultery, Jesus questioned her and listened to her testimony before making a judgment (John 8:1-11), breaking the legal taboo that women could not act as witnesses in a court of law because their word was unreliable. When a woman who was a known sinner washed His feet with her tears and wiped His feet with her hair (Luke 7:36-50), Jesus destroyed the belief that women shouldn't receive blessings by publicly forgiving her. Mary Magdalene, Mary (the mother of James), Joanna, Susanna, and others traveled with Him (Luke 8:3; Mark 15:40-41), smashing the custom of women remaining secluded at home. Finally, He talked to the woman at the well (John 4:7-26), destroying the cultural taboo that men were not to speak to women in public.

Jesus also included women in the central events of His ministry. As promised by God to Eve, He was born of a woman (Luke 2:5-7). When He was presented at the temple, Anna, a prophetess, spoke of Him to those who were looking for the redemption of Jerusalem (Luke 2:36-38). Women were present at His crucifixion (John 19:25) and were the first to witness His resurrection (John 20:1-18). Both the risen Lord and an angel then gave them the incredible responsibility of telling the disciples about His resurrection (Matthew 28:1-10).

Jesus' trust in women proved to be well founded. As Dr. Jim Davis and Dr. Donna Johnson state in their book,[17]

there is no instance of a woman in the gospels being an enemy of Jesus. No woman deserted or betrayed, persecuted or opposed Him. But women followed Him, they ministered to Him of their substance, they washed His feet with tears, they anointed His head with spikenard and ... they accompanied Him with weeping and wailing to the scene of martyrdom.

In an act that was as agonizing as it was amazing, Jesus suffered and died for their sins, delivering women from condemnation and blame and setting them free. His sacrifice for them restored them to their original position: innocent and equal. He freed them from the unjustified blame and inferior status that had been heaped upon them.

This change concerning the status and role of women was astonishing and inconceivable to first-century Jewish society. This tearing down of the cultural traditions concerning women was one more way in which Jesus revealed God's kingdom to the world. In particular, raising women to be acknowledged as *bona fide* ministers at the same level and in the same positions as men was a

[17] Davis, Jim, and Donna Johnson. *Redefining the Role of Women in the Church; A Mandate for the Apostolic Reformation,* Christian International Ministries Network, 1997, p. 58.

declaration that the old cultural and religious taboos were to end and a new cultural and religious norm was to begin.

Jesus' advocacy of women was nothing less than revolutionary. The old order of exclusion was to end, and a new order of inclusion was to begin. As He raised women to public positions of prominence and responsibility, it was His firm intention that His example would move men's hearts to do so as well.

That Jesus won this war is seen in the fruit of His ministry. Women were given place in leadership and authority and became prominent in the early Church. Mary, the mother of John Mark, had the first home Church (Acts 12:12). Lydia, the first European convert, founded the Church in Philippi (Acts 16:14-15, 40). Others prayed and prophesied. Phoebe served as a deacon in the church at Cenchrea (Romans 16:1), and one unnamed woman was an elder (2 John 1).

Women were also active in the five-fold ministry (Ephesians 4:11). Junia was an apostle in Rome (Romans 16:7). St. John Chryostom, a prominent archbishop of the late fourth century who was known for denouncing the abuse of authority within both the Catholic Church and the Roman Empire, recognized Junia's apostolic authority and said of her, "Oh how great is the devotion of this woman that she should even be counted worthy of the appellation of apostle."[18] Phillip's daughters and Anna were respected prophetesses (Acts 21:8-9; Luke 2:36-38 respectively). The woman at the well and the women sent to tell the disciples that Jesus had arisen from the dead were early evangelists (John 4:7-42; Matthew 28:5-8 respectively). Chloe, Nympha, and Prisca/Priscilla were pastors (1 Corinthians 1:11; Colossians 4:15; Romans 16:3-5 respectively). In these passages, local churches or fellowships being described as meeting in their

[18] Bristow, John Temple. *What Paul REALLY Said About Women: The Apostle's Liberating Views on Equality in Marriage, Leadership, and Love,* Harper One, 1991, p. 57.

homes indicates that they were the leaders or overseers of them. Finally, Priscilla was also a well-known teacher who taught Apollos, another prominent preacher and teacher (Acts 18:26). It is worthy of note that in both Acts 18:26 and Romans 16:3-5 Priscilla's name is listed before her husband, Aquilla's. In first-century Roman culture, the person who has the most honor or distinction would be the first in a list of names, so Priscilla is being given the higher distinction.

THE TRUTH

Jesus loved and valued women; He gave His life for them. His sacrifice at the cross for the forgiveness of sin did not exclude them. The blessings from the cross were not denied them. He suffered and died for **all**. To redeem **all**. To set **all** free. That includes women.

At one point in His earthly ministry, Jesus began to wash his disciples' feet (John 13:1-17). Meeting instant resistance from the astonished Peter, Jesus said to him, *"If I do not wash you, you have no part with Me"* (John 13:8). Given the green light to proceed, Jesus then accomplished His task, bathing the feet of His beloved followers. When finished, He said, *"Do you know what I have done to you? You call Me Teacher and Lord; and you are right, for so I am. For I gave you an example that you also should do as I did to you"* (John 13:13-15).

The application is clear. Many men and women in both the world and the Church have been soiled by walking in the defilement and filth of prejudice, hypocrisy, ungodly beliefs, and unholy behavior concerning women. It is time to let Jesus wash the feet of His twenty-first century disciples, granting Him permission to complete a thorough cleansing of their hearts and minds, so that all the grime, stain, stench, and ingrained filth is removed. Moreover, it is time to do exactly as He said to do. If He is Teacher and Lord, His disciples must follow His example and must do as He did:

love and honor women.

Chapter 7

THE GALATIANS CONTROVERSY

"[T]here is neither male nor female; for you are all one in Christ Jesus." (Galatians 3:28)

Approximately twenty years before Paul spoke the words quoted above, God's rock, Peter, began to pull back the veil that shrouded the truth about God's heart toward women. Soon after Jesus' death, burial, resurrection, and ascension, a defining moment ignited the new Church. In response to Jesus' injunction, *"not to leave Jerusalem, but to wait for what the Father had promised"* (Acts 1:4), both His male and female disciples had gathered *"all together in one place"* (Acts 2:1). While they were praying, suddenly and powerfully the Holy Spirit came upon them. So different, so amazing, so mighty was this event that it soon spilled out onto the streets of Jerusalem (Acts 2:6-12).

When Jews who were in Jerusalem from many other nations saw the sight and heard the sounds of the miraculous, they were confused, perplexed, and amazed. Peter, taking full advantage of the situation stood and began to speak in order to explain what was happening:

*For these are not drunk, as you suppose ... But this is what was spoken of by the prophet Joel: "And it shall come to pass in the last days," says God, "That I will pour out of My Spirit on **all** flesh; your sons **and your daughters** shall prophesy, your young men shall see visions, your old men shall dream dreams. And on My* *menservants **and on My maidservants** I will pour out My Spirit in those days; and they shall prophesy."* [emphasis added] (Acts 2:15-18 NKJV)

Many authors have justifiably declared that his statement is the Magna Carta of the Christian faith. It renounced the social, cultural, and religious degradation of women, and it raised them to a stature not previously enjoyed. It announced that women were as blessed as men were. It made them equal in Spirit to men. If prophecy means the speaking forth of God's will and the communication of religious truth under divine inspiration, these inspired words gave women the same authorization as men for proclaiming the counsel of God and the gospel of grace.

As the Magna Carta was to set the people of England free from the tyranny of an abusive king and to allow them to walk in new privilege, so Peter's declaration was to free both men and women from the oppressive religious establishment (whether Gentile or Hebrew) and to allow them to walk in the freedom God had given them. It set the stage and declared God's vision for the future of women in both their homes and the new Church. It also made provision for the active participation of men and women in the new move of God.

According to Peter, rather than being governed by Law, the body that was quickly forming into His Church would be led by Spirit. Rather than emphasizing a certain age group, it included young and old. Rather than being comprised of just the free, it included those who were servants or slaves. Finally, rather than being led and run exclusively by men, this new body would include women.

The reason for such an outpouring of power was that all disciples were to be witnesses of God even to the end of the earth (Acts 1:8). Further, these anointed ones were to prophesy (Acts 2:17-18) and to commit themselves to fellowship, communion, prayer, and praise (Acts 2:42-47).

Without question, God promised (Genesis 3:15), confirmed (Jeremiah 31:31-34), and then instituted a New Covenant with mankind that made the Mosaic Covenant obsolete (Hebrews 8:13). This new contract was founded on grace, not law, and was (and still is) centered in the spirit and heart of each man and woman rather than in buildings, rites, and rituals. Its High Priest is Jesus Christ, and its priesthood is composed of His disciples or of all who believe in and obey Him.

About thirty years after declaring that both men and women were to be active in ministry, Peter further enhanced the position of women in the Church. First, he pointed out that **all** believers were *"living stones ... being built up as a spiritual house for a holy priesthood"* (1 Peter 2:5). Then, he went on to proclaim them to be, *"a chosen race, a royal priesthood, a holy nation, a people for God's own possession"* (1 Peter 2:9). In neither of these verses did he include men but exclude women.

Though God intended that **all** saints be included in His holy priesthood, such is often not the case. Religious organizations and individuals have often severely restricted the activities of women in service unto God. In effect, while women are allowed to be members of His Church, they are often either barred from ministry entirely or their ministry is severely limited to such things as cleaning, providing food, and working with young children.

It is God's will that His Church follow holy rather than human traditions (Matthew 15:1-3) and obey God rather than men (Acts 5:29). In order to do this, the Church or assembly of born-again believers must know His Word, which reveals that God has never declared any gender-based restrictions on those called to serve Him in New Testament priesthood.

While Peter introduced this revolutionary change, the place and status of women have been greatly affected by the words of another apostle, Paul, in his epistles to the new

Church. While he intended to continue the policy of Jesus and to incorporate women into the Church, his words have been systematically and consistently misunderstood and mistranslated. As they appear in our Bibles now, his words do not accurately declare his intent. Yet, without being questioned or correcting the errors, they have been used for centuries as the basis for gender bias and for excluding women from their rightful roles in the home and in the Church.

At least three of Paul's biblical epistles contain controversial passages concerning women in the Church. These are found in Galatians 3, 1 Corinthians 11 and 14, and 1 Timothy 2. Further, both Paul and Peter wrote verses that have become controversial concerning women at home. These can be seen in Ephesians 5 and 1 Peter 3.

The first controversial Scripture concerning the position of women in the Church is Galatians 3:28: *"There is neither Jew nor Greek, there is neither slave nor free, there is neither male nor female; for you are all one in Christ Jesus."*

In order to understand these words better, it is necessary to understand the historical, cultural, and religious context in which they were written. Historically, Paul wrote the letter to the Galatians somewhere between 49 – 55 AD to refute the gospel of works, to defend the gospel of faith, to refute the idea that Gentile converts had to follow Jewish tradition, and to free people from the Law.

Culturally, it deals in part with the struggle to change ideas and habits concerning the identity and responsibility of women.

Religiously, under the Old Covenant, the priesthood was composed of Jewish, free males. In fact, under this religious system, only Jewish, free males were considered valid members of the religious community. So, when Paul wrote, *"There is neither Jew nor Greek, there is neither slave nor free, there is neither male nor female...."* (Galatians 3:28) he was declaring that the religious distinctions of the Old Testament were no longer valid. This was revolutionary.

Paul was announcing that the class and caste systems that had excluded the majority of society from worship had been blown to smithereens. He was revealing that what had once been legal grounds for division, separation, rejection, superiority, and exclusion no longer existed. The playing field had just been leveled.

Where the Law had declared differences, grace now abounded. The three classes that had been excluded from ministry to God under the old system, Gentiles, slaves, and females, were now to be included in religious activities if they belonged to Christ. Racial, social, and gender differences were irrelevant for those in right relationship to God. Spiritually, the sexes were equal; all could serve the Lord.

Paul was not guaranteeing worldly, humanist, radical dispensations to those who, twenty-one centuries later, want to catapult women into a position above men. Rather, he was simply but forcefully declaring that women in the Church have already been given total freedom in Christ to live productive, meaningful lives of ministry and worship in a way equal to that of men. Such liberty to move among, interact with, and minister alongside men is a blessing and a command of their salvation.

As Peter's words are considered the Magna Carta for women, so Paul's are dubbed the Emancipation Proclamation. His declaration is so powerful that it releases believing women from the degradation and abuse of a male-dominated religious society, reinstates them to the place and role intended for them from the beginning, and declares sexual equality before God.

THE TRUTH

As Galatians 3:28 makes clear, through God's grace and mercy, both men and women were born in the image of God and filled with the Spirit of God. This means that women were raised in stature to be the spiritual equal of men. Such elevation eliminated the tradition of hierarchy and established the principle of spiritual equality in the Church.

Chapter 8

THE CORINTHIANS QUESTIONS

"An excellent wife is the crown of her husband." (Proverbs 12:4)

While Galatians dealt with positional change, or the revelation that men and women were to enjoy spiritual equality, Paul's letters to the Corinthians dealt with social and cultural change, or the appearance and behavior of women, particularly within the fledgling Church. Several scriptures in 1 Corinthians are key to understanding what Paul said to that first-century Church community – and from then to the twenty-first century Church as a whole.

In order to better understand Paul's letter to the Church in Corinth, we first should look at the historical, cultural and religious setting. Historically, the letter to the Corinthian Church was written about 56 AD or a few years after Paul's epistle to the Galatians.

Culturally, Corinth was the most important city in Greece at that time, a bustling center of worldwide commerce. It was "the capital of Roman Greece, equally devoted to business and pleasure" and was known as a city of "luxury and vice."[19] The Church was struggling in its exodus from pagan society and Jewish tradition.

---

[19] "Ancient Corinth," *Sacred Destinations,* Sacred Destinations, n.d., http://www.sacred-destinations.com/greece/corinth. Accessed 21 Jun 2019.

Religiously, Corinth was full of pagan temples and shrines from which women were excluded. The exception to this was the myriad of temple prostitutes. For example, the temple of Aphrodite had 1,000 priestesses who were sacred prostitutes who plied their trade on the city streets every night.[20]

Paul's letters were written to address some of the more flagrant problems that had arisen in the Church members' lifestyles, to correct the carnal living practices (e.g. divisions, lawsuits, and immorality), and to address the problem of women in the Church. Due to their previous religious exclusion, when they were exposed to the Christian Church, neither Jewish nor Gentile women knew how to conduct themselves appropriately. Therefore, part of Paul's letter was to instruct them.

In 1 Corinthians, four topics have been and continue to be controversial. They are found in 1 Corinthians 11:3 (the controversy of the head), 1 Corinthians 11:4-6 (propriety in worship), 1 Corinthians 11:7-12 (Paul's version of Genesis); and 1 Corinthians 14:34-35 (order in the Church). In each of these verses, questionable translations of God's Word have led to great misunderstanding, which in turn has led to the wounding and abuse of women.

THE CONTROVERSY OF THE HEAD

"But I want you to understand that Christ is the head of every man, and the man is the head of a woman, and God is the head of Christ" (1 Corinthians 11:3). For centuries, this verse has been used to dominate women. Both in the Church and in the world, it has often been quoted to "put women in their place." Though it looks straightforward, is this verse really saying what it seems to be saying?

[20] "Ancient Corinth," *Sacred Destinations,* Sacred Destinations, n.d., http://www.sacred-destinations.com/greece/corinth. Accessed 21 Jun 2019.

The key to understanding the truth behind Paul's words lies in understanding the word head. The original Greek has two words for the one English word head. One of these is *arche* (746), which *Strong's Concordance* says means head in terms of leadership, as in the English words archetype and archbishop. Too, as seen in the words archangel and archenemy, *arche* means first in terms of importance or power or one who is the head, chief, or prince. *Arche* also means a beginning or a point of origin; from this comes our word archeology.

If, as Aristotle and human tradition has taught, husbands should command their wives and rule over them, Paul would have used this word to indicate that men were either to rule their wives or that man was the source of woman. Yet, he did not. Instead, he chose a different Greek word.

In this verse, Paul uses the word *kephale* (2776) for the word head. According to *Strong's*, it means head, top, or that which is uppermost in relation to something. Further, it denotes foremost in terms of position as a capstone over a door or the cornerstone of a foundation. *Kephale* can also be a military term describing one who goes before the troops, the one in the lead, or the first one into battle.

Although the word *kephale* signified the point man, it was never used to mean boss, ruler, dictator, or tyrant. It was never intended to be so misinterpreted and misunderstood that it was viewed as authorization for men to dominate women or for husbands to abuse their wives.

According to Paul, God was the *kephale* or Head of Christ when He was a Man among mankind. Christ is the *kephale* of humanity, the One uppermost in relationship with the creatures He created, the capstone and cornerstone of their Christianity, and the One who goes ahead and leads all men and women. The obvious example of this is Jesus as the Shepherd leading His flock (John 10:1-16).

Continuing in this vein, when Paul announced that men were the *kephale* rather than the *arche* of women, this Scripture is seen in a whole new light. He is not saying that men are permitted to intimidate, dominate, control, dictate to, or tyrannize women. He is saying that men are to act toward women as God acted toward Jesus and as Jesus acted toward mankind. That is, men are to be the head and to go before women in order to lead and protect them. Though he is the head, his hallmark is to have a servant's heart.

Thus, 1 Corinthians 11:3 has a dual purpose: it confirms to women that men are the head and it also defines to men exactly what kind of head they should be. The fact of male headship is not the real issue; rather the issue is what type of headship is indicated. By Paul's instruction, a woman is not subject to an *arche*, who has assumed dictatorial power over her, but to a *kephale*, who leads in love, protects with every beat of his heart, and guides by *agape* or an ongoing, outgoing, self-sacrificing concern for another. Therefore, by Paul's instruction, if a man is acting as an *arche* rather than a *kephale,* he is out of God's order, and a woman is under no obligation to submit to his abusive demands.

Women coming out of centuries of degradation and targeted abuse welcomed these instructions about their headship. While they grew and learned, such consideration from a *kephale* established biblical order and blessed them. Further, depending upon their choices, it had the potential to be a self-perpetuating mercy. The more they voluntarily submitted to honest, capable, protective, and loving leadership, the more men would want to lead after that fashion. This was not another denial of or removal of personal rights but a freedom to enjoy such rights. Women were in protective custody, so to speak.

Even today no biblical command demands a woman submits to (nor should she be willing to submit to) domination by an *arche* or suffer the abuse of a tyrant or dictator in her own home. Yet, almost any God-fearing woman would welcome submission to a *kephale* in her home, in the government, in her Church, or at her job. What better place to learn, mature, and be disciplined than in the sheltered environment of love – even while completing her husband and fulfilling the will of God?

PROPRIETY IN WORSHIP (OR THE CONTROVERSY OF THE HEAD COVERING)

Every man who has something on his head while praying or prophesying disgraces his head. But every woman who has her head uncovered while praying or prophesying disgraces her head, for she is one and the same as the woman whose head is shaved. For if a woman does not cover her head, let her have her hair cut off; but if it is disgraceful for a woman to have her hair cut off or her head shaved, let her cover her head. (1 Corinthians 11:4-6)

It must be understood that these verses are addressed to a particular people concerning a particular problem. They were written to Corinthian women who had never been to religious services before and didn't know what was or what was not appropriate.

In the first century, Greek men usually wore their hair short, while the women wore it long and bound up. The only women who wore short hair were prostitutes. The Jews also had their customs concerning hair. Though men could have long hair, most had short. Women wore their hair long and were required to bind it up. If any dared to wear it loose and flowing, they were considered to be loose women. The people of that culture understood that if a woman appeared publicly with her hair unbound, it meant that she was dishonoring her wedding vows.

As Bristow explains,[21] the problem was not so much

about the length of hair as how God was worshipped. Jewish men worshiped with their heads covered. They believed that the Shekinah glory of God surrounded and rested upon those men and women who pleased Him. In their minds, just as one might wear a hat for protection from the fierce sunlight, one should wear a hat when entering the brilliance of God's splendor. Therefore, it was an act of reverence and humility to wear a head covering during worship as Moses wore a veil to hide the radiance of his face after being in the presence of God (Exodus 34:29-35). Even today Jewish men still wear kippahs to show reverence to God.

First-century Greek men, on the other hand, found this custom strange and distasteful. Since hair length and head coverings meant different things to different people and cultures, Paul was trying to reconcile the situation among the Greeks and Jews who were joining the Church.

By the words quoted in 1 Corinthians 11:4-6, Paul tried to introduce an amicable way of dealing with the problem. He reminded Jewish men that their Head was not Moses but Christ, so if they were to cover their heads it might be interpreted as though they were ashamed of Christ or as if they were hiding from Him. Similarly, Paul did not want newly-freed women to be mistakenly viewed as prostitutes and thus to bring themselves and their new-found faith into question. Therefore, he urged them to keep their hair long and bound up. They were not to dishonor their head by cutting their hair short and by appearing as a pagan prostitute.

Seen in the context of two cultures trying to become one Church, the question in both cases was not really what Greeks or Jews and what men or women were to do with their hair. Rather, it had to do with what they were indicating by what they did with their hair.

[21] Bristow, John Temple. *What Paul REALLY Said About Women: The Apostle's Liberating Views on Equality in Marriage, Leadership, and Love,* Harper One, 1991, pp. 85-86.

While the problem dealt mainly with the cultural and social situation in the first century, it still has relevance today. Though customs have changed, the principles behind Paul's instructions still hold.

First, men should appear at worship services in ways that honor their Head, Christ. Too, women should appear in public in ways that honor both Christ and their heads, their husbands or leaders. Neither should appear in any way that would dishonor their *kephale*.

Next, men and women in the new Church were not to use their new freedom to cause offense. Paul did not want them deliberately or inadvertently to turn others against them or against the Church through their words or actions.

Lastly, Paul's words were meant to honor those to whom honor was due, not to rebel against social standards.

PAUL'S REVIEW OF GENESIS

For a man ought not to have his head covered, since he is the image and glory of God; but the woman is the glory of man. For man does not originate from woman, but woman from man; for indeed man was not created for the woman's sake, but woman for the man's sake ... However, in the Lord, neither is woman independent of man, nor man independent of woman. For as the woman originates from the man, so also the man has his birth through the woman; and all things originate from God. (1 Corinthians 11:7-12)

In these verses, Paul is trying to undo some damage. At the time this letter was written, it was taught that God had created man after His image, but woman had been created from the side of man and therefore after man's image, not God's. Further, it was taught that because of Eve's sinful actions, all women were cursed.

Since he knew differently, Paul was trying to introduce a new perspective, one that would introduce the truth and would change opinions about women. He did so in four sweeping statements.

First, in verse 7, he declared that women were the glory of men. That is, they were not an afterthought, not forever cursed or damned by God, and not objects created for the use and abuse of men.

Second, in verse 9, by reiterating that Eve had been created for Adam's sake because it was not good for man to be alone, Paul was stating that woman had been formed as a direct result of man's need. In other words, the man had a deep need and God's solution was the woman.

Third, when Paul wrote verse 11, it was in the context of public prayer or worship. He was opposing the pagan practice of excluding women from their religious services and the Jewish practice of segregating and silencing women during their religious services. Instead, Paul is affirming that in worship, men and women need each other. One of the key phrases in this verse is *"in the Lord."* While acting as representatives of the kingdom of God, men and women are not independent of each other; rather, they are interdependent. Since both are from the Lord, when in the Lord, neither can fully honor the Lord without the other.

Finally, in verse 12, Paul demolishes the traditional beliefs about the inferiority of women because they originally came out of man. Without question, the original woman came out of the original man. Yet, ever since, every single man has come out of a woman. So, it logically follows that if being drawn out of man makes women inferior to men, then so also each man is inferior to his mother because he was drawn out of her. Yet, Paul reminds us that when all is said and done, we should keep in mind that all things, including men and women, originate from God.

ORDER IN THE CHURCH

Gentile and Jewish women who had not before been allowed to participate in religious services did not know how to respond to their new freedom. They did not know what behavior was appropriate and what was inappropriate. Due to their ignorance, some behavior problems arose which Paul addressed:

> *The women are to keep silent in the churches; for they are not permitted to speak, but are to subject themselves, just as the Law also says. If they desire to learn anything, let them ask their own husbands at home; for it is improper for a woman to speak in church.* (1 Corinthians 14:34-35)

As the verses in 1 Corinthians 11 had to do with appropriate appearance in Church, so these in 1 Corinthians 14 have to do with appropriate behavior. Despite what has been taught through the ages, they are **not** an across-the-board demand for the silencing of women.

Human Tradition

There are two areas of controversy in this passage. The first is quickly resolved. Amid the commands that seem to ban women from public utterance there appears the phrase, *"as the Law also says"* (1 Corinthians 14:34). To what law is this comment referring?

Though a prohibition against women speaking in the Church did not exist in the Law, it was forbidden in Jewish oral tradition. Though speaking out was not forbidden by God in His Word, it was banned by human tradition. Since new believers were not under the authority of this man-made standard, they were therefore under no obligation to obey it.

Mistranslated And Misunderstood Words

The other area of controversy concerning 1 Corinthians 14:34-35 again involves the mistranslation and misunderstanding of words. In these verses, several Greek words appear that merit further study. Three of these, women, silent, and speak, will be dissected in the next few pages. The larger subject of submission will be addressed in chapters nine and ten.

Again, the Gentile and Jewish women, who had not before been allowed to be part of religious services, did not know how to respond to their new freedom. Due to their behavioral problems, they had become such a source of disorder that Paul was seeking to correct them. He was not commanding women to be muzzled or to be forced into silence nearly all the time; instead, he desired them to be quiet voluntarily at certain times.

Women

The first word that is key to understanding Paul's word is women. His specific choice to indicate the female gender is *gune* (1135). While this noun does mean a woman, *Strong's Concordance* is clear that it indicates a particular woman – the specific wife of a specific husband. Therefore, while these verses reveal proper relationship between a husband and wife, they are **not** an indication of or permission for males in general to boss, to dominate, to dictate to, to put down, or to have authority over females in general.

Silent

The second questionable word has probably caused the most confusion and tension between women and men. Just as importantly, it has caused confusion and tension between women and the Church. That is the word for silent.

The ancient Greek has three words for silent. One of these is *phimoo* (5392), and *Strong's Concordance* says it means to tie shut, to muzzle, or to forcibly silence someone. In the English vernacular, this means, "SHUT UP!" Jesus used *phimoo* to command the unclean spirit He was casting out of a man to keep quiet (Mark 1:25).

Another Greek word for silent is *heushia* (2237), which *Strong's* defines as having a calm, peaceful demeanor or to maintain a serene, restful spirit.

However, Paul does not choose either of these words when he commands women to be silent. Instead, he uses the word *sigao* (4601), which means to willingly hold one's peace, according to *Strong's Exhaustive Concordance of the Bible*. It means silence asked for amid disorder and clamor. It describes an internal, voluntary silence, not an external, enforced command. This word was exampled by Jesus when He was silent in His trial before Pilate (Mark 14:61) and by the crowd which told the beggar to be quiet when he was crying out for Jesus (Luke 18:39).

Speak

The third word causing problems in these verses is speak. In the Greek, five words mean to preach or proclaim, and Paul used none of these five words in telling women not to speak. According to Bristow, Paul was not and still is not indicating that women "are not to preach, or teach, or declare, or give a discourse, or proclaim, or affirm, or aver, or speak for something, or any other of the distinctive meanings found in many of those verbs." [22]

---

[22] Bristow, John Temple. *What Paul REALLY Said About Women: The Apostle's Liberating Views on Equality in Marriage, Leadership, and Love,* Harper One, 1991, p. 63.

Rather, when Paul said women were not to speak, he used the word *laleo* (2980). *Strong's Concordance* states that this word means they were not to idly chat, to talk out loud and cause confusion, or to talk randomly. By so doing, he was teaching women not to disrupt the Church service. Or, if they didn't understand something, he was telling them to hold their peace until they got home, where they could ask for and receive instruction and understanding from their husbands. Women new to Church society needed to understand that a Church meeting was not a social hour or a time to catch up on the news. Instead, it was a time to honor God, so they should willingly be silent during this time.

These verses do not reintroduce gender bias in the Church, which can be seen in their context. They follow Paul's instruction that when *"the whole church assembles together and **all** speak in tongues … **all** prophesy … **each one** has a psalm, has a teaching, has a revelation, has a tongue, has an interpretation…."* [emphasis added] (1 Corinthians 14:23-26). In every case, the words all and each includes the women. Therefore, if Paul here gives women permission to participate verbally in the religious services, it is ludicrous to suggest that just a few verses later he reverses himself by saying women cannot speak or take part in those same services.

Also, please note 1 Corinthians 14:28 where Paul speaks of the Church members keeping silent if there is no interpreter for a message in tongues and 1 Corinthians 14:30 where he speaks of prophets keeping silent so all can have a chance to talk. In these two verses, Paul again uses the word *sigao* to indicate a voluntary restraint from speaking or to yield for a time so that others can interact. Since he does not mean that these speakers are to be muzzled or forced to be silent, he also does not mean that when referring to women speaking in church meetings, then or now.

THE TRUTH

These verses from 1 Corinthians explain that while women could and should participate in religious services, order had to be maintained. Women were to look appropriate when they left their homes so that others did not question their (and thus the Church's) reputation. Further, they were not to disrupt or disregard a service with chatter or idle gossip or to interrupt the service with questions or comments. Instead, they were to acknowledge the privilege of being part of the service by maintaining a voluntary silence and by paying attention.

Chapter 9

THE TIMOTHY TROUBLE: THE EDUCATION OF WOMEN

"A woman must quietly receive instruction with entire submissiveness. But I do not allow a woman to teach or exercise authority over a man, but to remain quiet."
(1 Timothy 2:11-12)

While verses in Galatians deal with the status of women and passages in 1 Corinthians give instruction on needed social changes, the difficult verses in 1 Timothy are concerned with the education of women.

Again, some background is helpful. Historically, 1 Timothy was written by the apostle Paul about 62 AD. At this perilous time in Church history, persecutions under Nero were about to begin, and Christian women would not be excluded from torture and death. When trouble came, they were killed along with men or forced into prostitution at pagan temples.

Culturally, neither Gentile nor Jewish women were educated, except for learning basic household tasks. Yet, in becoming Christians, they had been given new freedom in Christ to be instructed and to learn.

Religiously, though the Church in Ephesus began as a Jewish group, after splitting from the synagogues, it became a mixed group of Gentiles and Jews. This introduced a monumental clash of thoughts and practices. In addition, the practice of magic (Acts 19:19) and the presence of idols were widespread throughout the Roman Empire and were causing problems in the Church even at this early date. A third area of contention was that the Jewish converts were demanding that the Gentile converts follow Jewish ways, but the Gentiles wanted to retain their freedom. When Paul penned this letter to Timothy, who was in Ephesus at the time, His intent was to help, counsel, and guide Timothy.

The Church at Ephesus had to be put right. Knowing that ignorance on the part of unschooled women was in large part to blame for the problems that were affecting the new body of believers, Paul spoke forth strongly. In words that ring out with strength and authority even today, he wrote, *"A woman must quietly receive instruction with entire submissiveness"* (1 Timothy 2:11).

Without question, women were to be taught the doctrines of the new Christian faith. Just as importantly, while women were not to be stifled educationally, they were to be taught what was appropriate in a way that was appropriate. Like his words to the Galatians and the Corinthians, this too was a revolutionary concept, one completely foreign to both Greek and Jewish practice or custom. Even as he gave the command to allow women to be educated, so also he detailed the process of this instruction. First, a woman was to learn *"quietly."*

Recalling the earlier study in 1 Corinthians 14:34-35, there were several words in Greek for the words quiet or silence. When giving information about educating women here in 1 Timothy, Paul did not choose the word *phimoo*, which means to muzzle or to enforce silence. Nor did he choose the word *sigao*, which means to hold your peace voluntarily or to be silent in the midst of clamor in order to hear what the speaker is saying. Instead, for this situation he used the word *hesuchia* (2237). According to *Strong's Concordance,* this means that women were to learn in quietness of spirit. Restful meditation, studiousness, silence, and quietness were to be hallmarks of their attitude and comportment while they learned.

When *hesuchia* is used in 2 Thessalonians 3:12, its meaning and application are obvious. Paul said, *"Now such persons we command and exhort in the Lord Jesus Christ to work in quiet fashion and eat their own bread."* No one understood this to mean that new believers were to maintain complete silence while working or eating.

It follows that *hesuchia* is not a command for the complete silence of women in the Church either. Paul's words in 1 Timothy were not a ban on women speaking in the Church then or now. Rather, they were an instruction on manners. He was explaining that women who were in the process of being educated were not to interrupt those teaching them, to speak out of turn, or to disrupt the others who were trying to learn, too.

Next, women were to learn *"with entire submissiveness."* In introducing the vastly important topic of submission, it is necessary to understand that the word submission can be translated different ways depending on the tenses and endings of the Greek word *hupotassomai* (5293). *Strong's Concordance* informs us that these translations include to subject oneself, to place oneself under submission, to be respectful of, voluntary willingness to be responsive to the needs of others, or consideration of others.

In Galatians 3:28, though Paul had declared spiritual equality, there were still physical, functional, and positional differences between the genders. The men in leadership and the women in the process of being discipled were spiritually equal in Christ even though their functions and positions were varied.

Similarly, there were differences between the teachers and pupils. If a woman wanted to learn, she was to be submissive to her teachers in doing so. Like Paul, who sat and learned at the feet of the famous Jewish teacher Gamaliel (Acts 22:3), women were to submit to their instructors' words and ways. Further, they were to be consciously considerate of others in the class.

In other words, just as women had to learn how to behave while worshipping in a Church meeting, so also they had to learn how to conduct themselves while learning. Since they were not used to listening, learning, and thinking through doctrines or concepts, they didn't know how to study. It was of primary importance for them to learn that a classroom was not a social club but a place where order was expected and silence and submission was required.

Paul's next words, *"I do not allow a woman to teach"* (1 Timothy 2:12) seem to contradict his other statements concerning the education of women. For example, Paul supported Priscilla, as she taught others, including Apollos, a prominent, male, Christian speaker (Acts 18:24-26).

Therefore, it is logical to conclude that this verse was not an across-the-board prohibition against women teaching. Rather, it was a ban on certain women teaching in the Church at Ephesus. In making this statement, Paul was referring to the list of problems that the Ephesian Church was experiencing and was saying that women who were still immature Christians and who had not yet progressed past these errors were not eligible to teach. The apostle was not declaring that all women should not teach, just those who didn't know Scripture, the Christian message, or Christian doctrine. Basically, if they didn't know what they were talking about, they were not eligible to teach. The principle was not that all women were forbidden from teaching but that unlearned, unschooled women could not teach.

1 Timothy 2:13-14 confirms this concept. Adam was created first, and God informed him that he was forbidden to eat from the tree of the knowledge of good and evil (Genesis

2:15-17). Eve was created later, was ignorant of what God had decreed about this tree, and was deceived by the serpent. Paul didn't want that situation to be repeated; he didn't want saints to be ignorant of what God had said or for them to be deceived. Further, Paul didn't want immature or false teachers to instruct the saints using wrong or unscriptural views or commands. So, in these verses Paul is not declaring women unfit to minister as teachers. Rather, he is simply reiterating that because women were in large part still ignorant, men would have to teach them to keep them from falling into error.

One more point is salient in these verses. Having addressed the issues of silence, submission, and qualification, Paul nears the end of his instruction about the education of women with the words, *"I do not allow a woman to … exercise authority over a man"* (1 Timothy 2:12).

This Greek word for authority is *authentoo* (831). According to *Strong's Exhaustive Concordance of the Bible,* it means to domineer, to act on one's own authority, to dominate in an autocratic fashion, or to rule in rudeness.

These verses are in reference to an assembly where male and female, or, more accurately, husband and wife, are interacting. Paul is revealing that a woman should live a life that is above reproach and should not undermine, weaken, or thwart her husband's role in the Church or in the kingdom of God. He is stating that a wife should never intrude on or appropriate her husband's position in ministry or overstep her own God-given boundaries at his expense.

According to Jack Hayford, a well-known and highly respected pastor of pastors,

> A more valid understanding of submission shows a wife who says what she thinks in a very honest and open way, not badgering or demanding, and with a "gentle and quiet spirit" (1 Peter 3:4). Then she trusts

God to help her husband understand the value of partnership, to see they are co-heirs in the life of God (see Romans 8:16-17), and to respond appropriately.

Serenity and submission are not characterized by misty-eyed pacifism, but by the fruit of the Spirit, love, joy, peace and so on. A woman is not to insist on her rights. Yet, she should be free to express herself in a gracious way, as she feels led. If her husband does not receive what she says, she must look to the Lord to take up her cause. [23]

This passage of Scripture ends with famous words that have been infamously mistranslated and misinterpreted. *"Nevertheless she will be saved through childbearing if they continue in faith, love, and holiness with self-control"* (1 Timothy 2:15 NKJV).

In other writings, Paul has made it abundantly clear that salvation is a blessing of God granted to **any** who confess their sins and who receive forgiveness for them through the sacrifice of Jesus Christ. It is a transaction of grace through faith (Romans 4; Ephesians 2:8; 2 Thessalonians 2:13). Therefore, in 1 Timothy 2:15, Paul is **not** implying that women have a separate path to salvation from men. Women are not saved by works any more than men are. More specifically, women are not saved by the labor involved in bearing children.

In fact, the childbearing Paul is referring to in this Scripture is not the act of pregnancy and birth of millions of women through the ages; instead, it is a reference to Genesis 3:15. In *Young's Literal Translation of the Bible*, this is more accurately written: *"she [woman] shall be saved through **the** child-bearing"* [emphasis added] (1 Timothy 2:15). That is, men and women would ultimately be saved

[23] Hayford, Jack. "A Woman's Place in Christ," *Jack Hayford Ministries,* n.d., https://www.jackhayford.org/teaching/articles/a-womans-place-in-christ/. Accessed 12 Sep 2019.

and redeemed and brought back into spiritual relationship by the birth of the Babe, the Savior of the world, Emmanuel, God with us, Jesus Christ.

As Katharine Bushnell said,

Women are not saved from death in childbirth, nor are they spiritually saved merely by the animal process of giving birth to children. Women are saved from their sins and are saved for heaven precisely on the same terms as men, and on no additional terms; for God is no respecter of persons. What Paul says here, as literally translated from the Greek, is "She [woman] shall be saved by the childbearing" – that is, by the birth of a Redeemer into the world.[24]

THE TRUTH

Paul never intended his instructions to Timothy to unleash a cascade of venom concerning the teaching and instruction of women in the Church and the teaching and instructing by women in the Church. When his words are not mistranslated or misunderstood, they clearly make the case that women were and are to participate in Church services and were and are to learn in quietness and submission to those who would teach them. Further, when properly taught and trained, women were and are to take their place beside other believers preaching, teaching, prophesying, and declaring the Christian message.

---

[24] Bushnell, Katharine. *God's Word To Women*, God's Word To Women, 2005, p. 160.

Chapter 10

THE EPHESIANS DILEMMA

"….always giving thanks for all things in the name of our Lord Jesus Christ to God, even the Father; and be subject to one another in the fear of Christ."
(Ephesians 5:20-21)

While the letter to the Galatian Church revealed the spiritual equality of women and men, the letter to the Corinthians addressed social dilemmas, and the letter to Timothy dealt with the education of women, the letter to the Ephesians gives a glimpse of life as it was designed to be lived between husband and wife. In this epistle, the situation needing attention is not about men and women in general but about married couples. It is not about public worship or cultural change but about relationships within private homes.

Historically, this epistle was written in 61 or 62 AD when Paul was imprisoned in Rome. During an early missionary journey Paul traveled to Ephesus. Later, he returned and remained there for two years, so he had strong ties to this Church.

Culturally, this city was Greek in appearance and in culture. Ephesus was the location of the infamous temple to Artemis, with its hundreds of temple-prostitute priestesses. Yet, in this pagan stronghold, a growing number were becoming Christians. As with any newborns, they were immature in the Lord and were having trouble accepting all the blessings of God. To help them, Paul instructed them on such topics as walking after the Spirit, the unity of the faith, the five-fold ministry, spiritual warfare, and the armor of God.

Further, Paul sought to introduce a new way of honoring God. He was aware that the relationships of Gentile husbands and wives were based on Aristotle's idea that women were inferior and the relationships of Jewish husbands and wives were based on blaming women after the fall of Adam and Eve. Rather than supporting either of these flawed systems of male dominance, Paul worked to institute a new order. He wanted the relationship of husbands and wives to reflect Christ and the Church, a marriage where men and women are content under their headship and are voluntarily interrelated in service, mutual care, and concern for each other. To gain this end, he wrote:

> Wives, be subject to your own husbands, as to the Lord. For the husband is head of the wife, as Christ also is head of the church; He Himself being the Savior of the body. But as the church is subject to Christ, so also the wives ought to be to their husbands in everything. (Ephesians 5:22-24)

In these words, Paul is not advocating the suppression of females. Nor is he saying that headship equals domination. Rather, he is saying that the key to submission is not force or the coercion of the physically weaker by the physically stronger; it is love. To glean all of this, correct translation and proper understanding of the key words is essential.

The first of these all-important words is submit. In the Greek, several words mean to be subject to in English. One of these is *hupakouo*, and *Strong's Concordance* says this word indicates dutiful obedience. Examples of this type of submission are seen in the relationships of a child to a parent or a slave to a master. Another choice is the word *peitharcheo*. Since the word *arche* is found in its spelling, it means obedience to someone who is in authority. A biblical example of this is found in Acts 5:29 where Peter and the other apostles answered the high priest and the council with the words: *"We must obey God rather than men."* (See also Acts 27:21 and Titus 3:1.)

However, the word Paul uses here is not a command to obedience. The word he chooses to indicate submission is *hupotassomai* (5293). According to *Strong's Concordance*, in its active form, this word is used of a conqueror concerning the vanquished. It means to subject to or to subordinate. If Paul had used the active form of this word when he wrote God's heart concerning submission between men and women, it could be quite properly understood to mean that men are to dominate women.

Yet, Paul uses this word in the imperative form, not the active form. Understood correctly, it does not imply a subservient position. Submission is not to be something men do to women or are empowered to enforce upon them. It is not holy permission to subjugate their wives or to subject them to every male whim, caprice, or demand. Rather, submission is something women do. It is a choice given to them that they may freely and voluntarily accept or decline.

Since submission is intended to be a choice, women are not being forced to obey men but are being requested to subject themselves or to place themselves in submission to them. Since Paul begins Ephesians 5:22-24 with *"Wives,"* it is obvious that he is addressing women, not men. Therefore, he is not giving husbands permission to rule, control, dominate, abuse, or tyrannize their wives. Further, he is not commanding women but appealing to them. He is emphasizing the voluntary nature of becoming subject to their husbands or of being willing to tend to them, to give allegiance to them, to be supportive of them, to be responsible to them, and to yield to them.

A second word worthy of study in these verses is own. The Greek word for own is *idios* (2389). *Strong's* informs us that *idios* means that which is properly one's own. It pertains to a private person, not a public one, or a particular person rather than a general class or group. *Idios* signifies one apart from others of the same kind, one distinguished from the others, or one person alone. Ephesians 5:22-24 declares that a wife is to submit to her own husband only. She is not required to submit to anyone else's husband or to submit to men in general.

Seen from the opposite perspective, this passage also declares that no man has marital authority over any woman who is not his wife. Similarly, groups of men or men in general do not have authority over a man's wife; only her husband does. Her husband alone is her head. A wife is to have allegiance to her husband alone, to distinguish him above others, and to give him place of honor.

The third word of concern in these verses is head. Though this word *kephale* has been discussed in chapter eight, it is worthy of further study. The use of the word *kephale* means that the head of woman is the physical head or the one at the top, the one in the foremost position, the director, the one who goes before, or the leader. It never infers or implies one who is boss, ruler, master, or controller. First-century culture had dictated that women had to submit to men and social tradition commanded their compulsory subservience to male power. However, Paul is now emphasizing the voluntary action of women in submission. He is also deemphasizing forceful domination by men. Quite simply, Paul is declaring that God placed husbands as head over their wives and that it is good policy for wives to come under that blessing in an orderly fashion by submitting to them.

If Paul had used the word *arche* for head, which denotes head in terms of importance and power as a master, ruler, or dominator, then husbands would have had the right – even the responsibility – to control their wives and to enforce obedience. Yet, since he uses *kepale*, he is **not** indicating the total control of husbands over their wives or the enforced servility of wives.

Yes, Paul wants women to voluntarily come under the lead of their husbands, the ones who go before; to allow themselves to be led by the ones God placed in the position of head; and to respond favorably to the ones who are first into battle or the ones who sticks their necks out for them. Yet, nowhere does Paul command women to obey an abuser of God's holy order.

In fact, when husbands dominate their wives; when they dictate all aspects of their lives, including meddling in their choices of clothing and friends, deciding whether or not their wives can have a job outside the house; choosing what they can eat; decreeing where they can and cannot go; controlling their finances; forcing or refusing sexual encounters; or abusing them physically or mentally is to rob them of their personhood. Husbands are not to manipulate or abuse their wives, and they are not to prevent their wives from making their own decisions freely. It is of great importance that husbands should choose to act like God, who gives all women free will and then loves them into choosing submission, rather than to act like Satan, who denies free will and forces people to obey him through terror, manipulation, and coercion.

Paul then seeks to drive home the point that men need to go through a cultural shift and to lead in a manner different than those whose poor leadership example is to, *"lord it over them"* (Matthew 20:25). Speaking to married men, he reveals that the relationship between husbands and wives should be reciprocity. *"Husbands, love your wives, just as Christ also loved the church and gave Himself for her"* (Ephesians 5:25).

In this verse, Paul's word for love is *agape*. Recall that *agape* is ongoing, outgoing, self-sacrificing concern for another; it is love without condition and shown through actions. Therefore, a woman "being subject to" her husband is almost identical in meaning to a husband *agape*-ing or loving his wife. Both involve giving up self-interest to serve and care for another. Both mean being responsive to the needs of the other.

Paul highlights this idea of mutual love and submission within a marriage through a powerful statement that begins the topic in Ephesians 5: *"be subject **to one another** in the fear of Christ"* [emphasis added] (Ephesians 5:21). This verse was a radical departure from the usual marriage custom, but it is the way God desired the husband/wife relationship to function.

THE TRUTH

Paul's teaching in Ephesians 5 that wives are only subject to their own husbands and that submission between a husband and wife is to be mutual has been forgotten, ignored, denied, or twisted through the centuries. Neither marriage partner is sanctioned to dominate or control the other. In fact, both are to give up their own self-interest for the care and concern of the other, to tend to, to complete, to yield to, to care for, and to love each other as Christ, the head of the Church, so loved the Church.

Chapter 11

PETER WEIGHS IN

"Likewise you wives, be submissive to your own husbands...." (1 Peter 3:1)

Peter had become the head of the newly emerging Church. Along with the position came apostolic authority. His words, though spoken in difficult times, did indeed carry weight.

Historically, his first letter was written about 64 AD. Rather than being addressed to a specific Church, it was written to *"the pilgrims of the dispersion"* (1 Peter 1:1 NKJV). Culturally, throughout the Roman empire, hostility had been slowly growing against Christians and their new and different lifestyle and worldview. Christians were mocked for their way of life and scorned for their belief in one God. Then, on July 19, 64 AD, Rome burned. When the temples, shrines, and homes of the pagan empire had been destroyed, people were angry. Needing a scapegoat to blame for the conflagration, Nero pointed his finger at the blameless Christian community. As a result, the Roman government, which had previously tolerated the new religion, then turned on it. Persecutions began, and the members of the Church in Rome were scattered throughout the world.

Into this age strode Peter, all bluster and brawn. With all else that must have been occupying his mind and needing his attention, he nevertheless did not ignore the situation regarding women. Instead, he made an apostolic pronouncement concerning women:

> *In the same way, you wives, be submissive to your own husbands so that even if any of them are disobedient to the word, they may be won without a word by the behavior of their wives, as they observe your chaste and respectful behavior. Your adornment must not be merely external – braiding the hair, and wearing gold jewelry, or putting on dresses; but let it be the hidden person of the heart, with the imperishable quality of a gentle and quiet spirit, which is precious in the sight of God. For in this way in former times the holy women also, who hoped in God, used to adorn themselves, being submissive to their own husbands; just as Sarah obeyed Abraham, calling him lord, and you have become her children if you do what is right without being frightened by any fear.* (1 Peter 3:1-6)

The good news is that the words of Peter agree with the earlier words of Paul. In the minds of two primary first-century apostles, the instruction and declarations about women were essentially the same: wives were to recognize and submit to their own husbands as *kephale*. Allowing their inner beauty, tranquility, and peace to be their testimony, wives were to recognize, honor, and submit voluntarily to their own husbands in order to win them to the Lord by their conduct.

The only word in these verses that have caused controversy is found in verse six. When Peter said, *"Sarah obeyed Abraham, calling him lord,"* he was introducing an additional thought after his pronouncement about the behavior of wives towards their husbands. His words refer to Genesis 18:12. Abraham and Sarah had just heard the momentous announcement that they were to be the parents of a son. Since both were well past childbearing age, Sarah laughed at this news. Though her skepticism was evident, her inner thoughts showed that she honored her husband,

and her words reveal that she called him master or lord. *"After I have become old, shall I have pleasure, my lord being old also?"* The rest of the story makes evident the fact that she obeyed him too, for they did indeed become the parents of a son and heir, Isaac.

It is important to note that though he is often misquoted, Peter did not command women to obey their husbands. He is in no way demanding servitude. In this passage, Peter used two different words to mean two different things. In 1 Peter 3:1, he chose *hupotassomai* to teach the proper attitude of a wife toward her husband. Remember that *hupotassomai* means to subject oneself, to place oneself under submission, to be respectful of, and to be responsive to the needs of others. To contrast, in 1 Peter 3:6, he selected *hupakouo* (5219), which means to heed or to conform to a command, to harken, be obedient to or obey, according to *Strong's Exhaustive Concordance.* Peter used *hupakouo* to describe and commend Sarah's obedience toward her husband. As such, Peter was saying her actions and attitude were godly examples for every wife to emulate, that wives should prefer or defer to their husbands.

Though this is the only time that the word *hupakouo* is used in the Bible to portray one wife obeying her husband, many have aggrandized it to mean that all wives must always obey their husbands. Some men perceive it as holy authority to command their wives' obedience and as permission to enslave them into carrying out their every wish.

However, if these misinterpreters would continue to read God's Word, His truth would be found in a subsequent passage. After Isaac had been born,

> *Now Sarah saw the son of Hagar the Egyptian, whom she had borne to Abraham, mocking. Therefore, she said to Abraham, "Drive out this maid and her son; for the son of this maid shall not be an heir with my son*

Isaac." (Genesis 21:9-10)

Upset at this, Abraham took the situation to God. God commanded more obedience, but this time a husband was to obey a wife. *"Whatever Sarah tells you, listen to her"* (Genesis 21:12).

Abraham complied; he obeyed the command of his wife. *"So Abraham rose early in the morning and took bread and a skin of water and gave them to Hagar, putting them on her shoulder, and gave her the boy, and sent her away"* (Genesis 21:14).

The Word of God clearly shows that there are times wives obey husbands and times husbands obey wives. God is the One whose voice must be heard and whose will must be honored. These can only be fulfilled by the combined obedience of husband and wife to Him and to each other.

Peter doesn't just leave it there. He also speaks to men about their behavior toward their wives.

> *You husbands in the same way, live with your wives in an understanding way, as with someone weaker, since she is a woman; and show her honor as a fellow heir of the grace of life, so that your prayers will not be hindered.* (1 Peter 3:7)

A different translation that uses words that better suit the original rendering might be:

> *Husbands, dwell with or reside together with [sunoikeo – 4924] your precious wife. Understand her and be aware of her [gnosis – 1108, from gingko – 1097]. Though, as a female [gunaikeios – 1134, also means wife], she is physically weaker than you are [skeuos – 4632], spiritually she is your equal. Therefore, bestow [aponemo – 632] honor and respect on her; revere and esteem her [times – 5092].*

She is a co-heir [suglkeronomou – 4798], a co-participant, or one who shares or partakes in the same measure that you do, in the grace or God's divine favor [charis – 5485], and one who shares or partakes in the same measure that you do in His gifts and blessings.

As wives were to submit to their own husbands, husbands were to love their own wives, to live with them, to grant them respect and esteem, and to recognize them as co-participants in the blessings and gifts of God.

Peter's teaching for husbands to live with and honor their wives complements Paul's teaching in Colossians 3:19 for husbands to *"love your wives...."* When these two teachings are brought together, a beautiful picture emerges:

First, Paul tells the husband to love his wife, while Peter tells the husband to dwell together with his wife. The husband cannot live with his wife as Peter says unless he loves her in the way Paul means. The love that the husband is commanded to have for the wife is not primarily sexual or emotional; it is a love that loves despite the response (or lack of it) in the one loved.

Next, the two responsibilities the husband has in the family are to live with his wife in an understanding way and to render to his wife the honor that is due her because she is his wife. To dwell together with his wife means that the husband must take his wife into every aspect of his life. This means he is to talk to his wife about, to receive her thoughts and advice about, and to consider how his words or actions will affect her in every area of his life. This includes his work, his friends, his hobbies, his car, his parents, his siblings, his children, his home, and his finances. There are to be no areas of his life where there are signs that say, "Private, husband only – wife keep out."

Third, the husband is to perform his two duties for a

spiritual purpose: *"so that your prayers will not be hindered"* (1 Peter 3:7). Any man who is not taking his wife into every aspect of his life and is not giving her the honor that is due her because she is his wife cannot communicate with her the way that God intended. Therefore, he cannot communicate with God properly either. To make sure that the channel of communication with God is open, the husband must make sure that the channel of communication with his wife is open. Only in this way can he both love his wife as God intended and manifest his headship properly.

THE TRUTH

Peter agreed with Paul that wives were to recognize and submit to their own husbands as *kephale*. He then added that husbands also had the responsibility of honoring their wives and of recognizing their standing as co-heirs of Christ.

Who can stand as staunch pillars of New Testament truth in their epistles as Paul and Peter? And who has greater apostolic authority than Peter and Paul? No one should question their words as they state again and again that while women may physically need nurturing and protection in the world, spiritually, they are equal with men in the kingdom of God.

DIFFERENCES BEING INTRODUCED

THE OLD TESTAMENT WAY	THE NEW TESTAMENT WAY
1. Females are inferior to men	1. Men and women are one in Christ
2. Men and women are separated in worship	2. Men and women are to lead in worship
3. Women can't learn	3. Women are to learn
4. Marriage is a distraction	4. Marriage is a gift from God
5. Men are to command, and women are to obey	5. Husbands and wives are responsible to each other
6. Prostitution, adultery, and homosexuality are OK because they are ancient, hallowed traditions	6. Sex is confined to marriage, and marriage is confined to one partner
7. Women are morally weak	7. Women are the glory of men
8. Women walk in the curse	8. Eve was not cursed

9. Eve was not forgiven; therefore, women are not forgiven

9. Eve was forgiven

10. Due to Eve's sin, dominion, authority, rule, and control belong to men

10. Leadership in love belongs to men

11. Servile, subjugated, perfect obedience is the lot of women

11. Voluntary submission is a gift to women

Chapter 12

FROM THE FIRST TO THE TWENTY-FIRST CENTURY

*"Let Us make man in Our image, according to Our likeness
... male and female He created them ... God saw everything
that He had made, and indeed it was very good."* (Genesis
1:26, 27, 31)

It would be nice to say that the liberty Jesus brought to women became a permanent part of life in the Church. However, it did not. Jesus sacrificed Himself for the forgiveness of sin (including those of women) and set an example of treating women with dignity and value. Further, the eminent apostles Paul and Peter taught and wrote letters to reiterate God's granting of freedom, stature, and authority to women in the first century. Unfortunately, it did not last long. The enmity that God had established between the serpent and the woman in Genesis 3:15 and the human failings of prejudice, blame, repression, and desire for power soon resurfaced.

According to John Temple Bristow, in the second century a common Jewish prayer was, "Praise God He has not created me a ... woman." Even worse, a woman was described in the Talmud as a "pitcher of filth."[25] Yet, the Gentile influence was just as crushing. Tertullian, who lived

---

[25] Bristow, John Temple. *What Paul REALLY Said About Women: The Apostle's Liberating Views on Equality in Marriage, Leadership, and Love,* Harper One, 1991, p. 20.

around 160 – 230 AD, is one of the first moral and dogmatic theologians of the Latin Church. Regrettably, he twisted Paul's writings to promote his own incorrect beliefs and to attack women. He wrote to women:

> Do you not know that you are [each] an Eve? ... You are the Devil's gateway: You are the unsealer of that [forbidden] tree: you are the first deserter of the divine law ... On account of your desert – that is death – even the Son of God had to die.[26]

A contemporary of his, Origen, also demeaned and belittled women. He declared: "Men should not sit and listen to a woman ... even if she says admirable things, or even saintly things, that is of little consequence, since they came from the mouth of a woman."[27] Another example comes from the third-century doctor and philosopher, Galen, who used his expertise to align the medical community against women. He stated: "The female is more imperfect than the male. The first reason is that she is colder. If, among animals, the warmer ones are more active, it follows that the colder ones are imperfect."[28]

The fourth century proved a testing time for the early Church. When Constantine declared his conversion to Christianity, the Church and the government of the Roman Empire became intertwined. Since many who joined this new, hybrid church did so to curry the emperor's favor or to avoid trouble, true worship of the Lord did not feature prominently in it. Those who sought a more devout lifestyle left the rituals of the empire's church and established monasteries where they could practice holiness in their own communities. Celibacy became a new way to honor God.

[26] Grady, J. Lee. *Ten Lies The Church Tells Women: How The Bible Has Been Misused To Keep Women In Spiritual Bondage,* Charisma House, 2000, p. 118.

[27] ibid. p. 50.

[28] ibid. p. 18.

During this time, the writings of a monk, Jerome, became well known. Under his pen, the Greek ideas of the inferiority of women came flooding back. Revised by him, the writings of Aristotle again were accepted as the mainstream view of women. To Jerome, women served a basic purpose but were inferior to men. "As long as woman is for birth and children, she is different from man as body is from soul. But if she wishes to serve Christ more than the world, then she will cease to be a woman and will be called a man."[29]

Even the most influential and well-known Church father of this era, Augustine, shared this poor view of women. His religious thoughts and theories were of such great impact that they changed theological thinking in history even as they do today. It would have been wonderful if a man of such stature had used the tools available to him to search out and present the truth about women, but he did not. Continuing the established vein that women were of low or no account, he pronounced: "What is the difference whether it is in a wife or a mother; it is still Eve the temptress that we must be aware of in any woman...."[30]

Sadly, Aristotle, the pagan Greek philosopher, and Augustine, the Christian theologian, two men who were and still are revered as giants in Western civilization, reinforced erroneous contempt, shame, scorn, and accusation of women. This gave and still gives leaders of the Christian faith reason to exclude women from ministering in the Church. Their refusal to follow the example set by their Lord, Jesus Christ, and their erroneous declarations and misleading interpretations of Paul's writings have produced a sexual bias that has promoted the mistreatment of women from that century to this.

---

[29] Grady, J. Lee. *Ten Lies The Church Tells Women: How The Bible Has Been Misused To Keep Women In Spiritual Bondage,* Charisma House, 2000, p. 136.

[30] ibid. p. 18.

In the sixth century, Christian leaders debated in France as to whether or not women had souls. In the thirteenth century, Thomas Aquinas, one of the most influential theologians in Church history, rose to prominence in the Roman Catholic Church. Combining Aristotle's thoughts and questionable Church beliefs, his words served to affirm and authorize male-dominated households and male-dominated leadership in the Church. Agreeing with Aristotle that women are "defective and misbegotten," he laid the blame for mankind's woes solely on women and refused to believe that women were made in the image of God. Further, he robbed women of their God-given identity and responsibility by describing them as little better than slaves.

Widening the scope of his ignorant and malicious beliefs and teachings, Aquinas also denigrated the function of women. To him, "The only way Eve could be a helper to Adam was in terms of 'the work of generation,' the female's ability to give birth to children."[31] Further, "She was not fitted to help man except in generation, because another man would have proved a more effective help in anything else."[32]

By the time of the Reformation, men's ideas still produced cultural bias against women. Even in the Church, renowned Protestant giants like John Calvin and Martin Luther continued to disparage females. Calvin said of them:

> Woman was created later to be a kind of appendage to the man on the express condition that she should be ready to obey him, thus ... God did not create two heads of equal standing but added to the man a lesser helpmate."[33]

---

[31] Bristow, John Temple. *What Paul REALLY Said About Women: The Apostle's Liberating Views on Equality in Marriage, Leadership, and Love,* Harper One, 1991, p. 116.

[32] ibid. p. 117.

[33] Davis, James, and Donna Johnson. *Redefining the Role of Women in the Church; A Mandate for the Apostolic Reformation.* Christian

Luther's remarks were even more damaging. With more than a hint of the "keep 'em barefoot and pregnant" theme, he taught:

> Men have broad shoulders and narrow hips, and accordingly they possess intelligence. Women have narrow shoulders and broad hips. Women ought to stay at home; the way they were created indicates this, for they have broad hips and a wide fundament to sit upon, keep house and bear and raise children.[34]

To make his thoughts quite clear, Luther also said: "Women must neither begin nor complete anything without man: Where he is, there she must be, and bend before him as before a master, whom she shall fear and to whom she shall be subject and obedient."[35]

Perhaps this final example of historical rhetoric by the thirteenth-century Franciscan monk Salimbene concerning women says it all:

> Woman was evil from the beginnings, a gate of death, a disciple of the serpent, the devil's accomplice, a fount of deception, a dogstart to godly labours, rust corrupting the saints … Lo, woman is the head of sin, a weapon of the devil, expulsion from Paradise, mother of guilt, corruption of the ancient law.[36]

In the course of history, a few did see women as valuable and as an integral part of both society and the Church. For example, the Puritans educated girls and the

International Ministries Network, 1997, p. 25.

[34] Grady, J. Lee. *Ten Lies The Church Tells Women: How The Bible Has Been Misused To Keep Women In Spiritual Bondage,* Charisma House, 2000, p. 152.

[35] ibid. p. 170.

[36] ibid. p. 118.

Quakers promoted full rights for women to preach and teach. However, from earliest times, the overwhelming attitude toward women has been that Eve was weak, was susceptible to Satan's seduction, and was an accomplice in causing Adam to sin. In addition, her female descendants (but not her male descendants!) have inherited her weak, sinful nature, so they have continued to need chastisement for the sin of their ancestor.

Even today, the virulent and hateful history, culture, and human traditions still dictate the attitude of some men toward women and are their justification for keeping women enslaved and abused at home and missing-in-action in the Church. Yet, God has provided a liberating word to all who will hear and heed it:

> It will come about after this that I will pour out My Spirit on **all** mankind; and your sons **and daughters** will prophesy, your old men will dream dreams, your young men will see visions. Even on the male and **female** servants I will pour out My Spirit in those days. [emphasis added] (Joel 2:28-32)

This Scripture from Joel reappears in the New Testament in Acts 2:17-18. There, it is both a confirmation that, in these last days, God will pour out His Spirit on **all**, on men and women, and an affirmation that He intends to use these anointed women in His Church to accomplish His will. If that is His stated intent, is it wise to stand in His way?

Considering these words, there needs to be an honest evaluation in the twenty-first century attitude and practice toward women. What is the attitude of the Church toward its women today? Does it reflect the way and intent of the world, and thus thwart the will of God, or the way and intent of the kingdom of God, and thus honor Him? Are women considered inferior in identity? Are women, who comprise approximately fifty percent of the population, being hindered in function? Are they refused the opportunity to serve God and so become like buried treasures (Matthew

25:14-30)? Are they, like Pharaoh's slaves, given a heavy workload but not given the means of authority by which to accomplish it?

Or, are women being given the place and opportunity to worship God through obedience and service according to His will, calling, and anointing in their lives?

Can any who have so yielded to God regret the healing ministry of Katherine Kuhlman? Can any downplay the integrity of Catherine Booth? Can any truly claim that Joyce Meyer hasn't blessed multitudes with her teachings? Can any deny that Mother Teresa accomplished an unparalleled work of love for God amongst the poorest of the poor? Dare any now hinder those following in these footsteps in Christ?

Rather than being like the unworthy servant who buried his master's talents, the twenty-first century Church of God must allow women with holy anointing to fulfill their God-given callings. It must use its Master's talents to bring increase into His kingdom. It must allow its hidden treasures, women, to serve.

Not only must the Church allow women to serve, but it must allow them to serve in whatever position God is calling them to. Contrary to prevailing opinion, women are not solely relegated to menial tasks. In older times, different understandings of authority tended to equate headship with superior rank and power over others. Thus, in the Church, higher authority (men) had the power to relegate women to the continuous role of drudgery rather than leadership. Yet, the truth is that all authority resides in God and comes from God, not man. God has created each individual, has provided him **or her** with talents and abilities, has given him **or her** a unique calling, and has given him **or her** some authority in a certain area of responsibility.

In addition, the Bible does not record jobs or ministries from which women are excluded. 1 Timothy 3:1-13 lists the qualifications for elders or overseers, but there is a curious and unfortunate mistranslation. Where most English Bibles begin, *"if any man aspires to the office of overseer...."* (1 Timothy 3:1), Paul's actual words are, *"if **any** desires the position of overseer...."* [emphasis added]. In truth, neither here nor in the complementary verses found in Titus 1:5-9 does the word man or men appear. Further, the Greek does not include a masculine pronoun or possessive or other grammatical specification that would suggest that Paul had only men in mind for these offices. Since Paul declared that **any** could aspire to become an overseer in the Church rather than specifically delineating these roles to men only, the Church today should follow his direction in this matter and should not prohibit women from serving in leadership positions.

THE TRUTH

With the dawn of history came the promise of redemption. Jesus was born of a woman. His sacrifice freed all who will accept it from the curse of the law; from sin; and from blame, guilt, and condemnation. Regarding women, Scripture underscores the magnitude of that liberation: *"There is neither male nor female"* (Galatians 3:28).

Despite human traditions and faulty beliefs that shout a contrary message, this means that, to God, men and women are equal spiritually. Without regard to gender, He has given gifts and callings to all, and He expects them to be fulfilled by all. He is no respecter of persons. Mankind, both men and women, would do well to emulate Him.

Chapter 13

SUMMARY

In the garden of Eden, God commanded man and woman to be fruitful and multiply and to exercise dominion over His creation. Since God is eternal (1 Timothy 1:17) and unchanging (Malachi 3:6), these commands are still in effect today. His Son, Jesus, paid the penalty for all sin and made it possible for redeemed men and women to do so.

In this century, in this Church, male and female saints are spiritually equal in the eyes of God through the sacrifice and redemption of Jesus Christ. They have been given the authority of His anointing and calling, and they are to work together in loving submission, mutual respect, and gracious accountability in order to fulfill the commands of God in the unique way He has created in them without the issue of gender hindering them.

"And in all the land there were no women so fair as the daughters of Job; and their father gave them inheritance among their brothers" (Job 42:15). If God considers the women He created as beautiful, and if He, the Father, has given them an inheritance among their brothers, the Church should not do any less.

EXAM ON THE BIBLICAL VIEW OF SUBMISSION

Directions: Fill in the blank with **T** for true or **F** for false.

1. _____ Since God created Adam first, Eve was created inferior to Adam. Thus, since she was the first and representative female, all females are inferior to males.

2. _____ God molded man out of the dirt from the ground and blew the breath of life into him, but He drew woman out of man. Therefore, man was created in the image of God and woman was created in the image of man.

3. _____ Woman was created as an afterthought and served no real purpose.

4. _____ A woman is accountable for the entrance of sin into the world.

5. _____ All women are daughters of Eve and all are like her – deceptive, weak, and drawing men into sin. They are to blame for all the sins in the world.

6. _____ Since women are naturally weak and evil, they must be put under strict control. They must be repressed, held down, and kept under male authority.

7. _____ Women don't have to bear Eve's sin, guilt, shame, and curse.

8. _____ Submission means someone imposing demands on another or controlling, dominating, and forcing compliance to his or her will.

9. _____ Submission involves a power struggle between men and women, with the male imposing his demands on the female or the husband on the wife.

10. _____ Submission means that a man is always in charge, that a man makes all the decisions, and that what he says goes. It's his way or the highway.

11. _____ Every woman must obey her husband in all things.

12. _____ Every woman must submit to her husband in all things.

13. _____ Every woman must submit to every man in all things.

14. _____ Only men are the priests of the homes. Therefore, they can make – and not be questioned about – all household decisions.

15. _____ Since men are in charge of the home, it is all right for them to abuse their wives.

16. _____ Since men are in charge of the home, it is all right for them to abuse their children.

17. _____ Women must have a male "covering" in order to minister.

18. _____ Wives are to submit to their husbands, but husbands are not to submit to their wives.

19. _____ The patriarchal view of submission or male domination from the top down is the correct one.

20. _____ There is a difference between submission and subjection.

21. _____ Submission can mean preferring or deferring to one another rather than dominating or ruling over one another.

22. _____ True submission is a Christlike model of servant leadership that empowers and releases into responsibility rather than controls or dominates.

23. _____ A man given to anger is not qualified to serve in ministry.

24. _____ The biblical word for submission carries with it the idea of identifying with, being attached to, or becoming one with. The issue here should be oneness and unity between partners, not the divisiveness of who controls whom.

25. _____ The words for submission and *agape* love are similar in meaning.

ANSWERS TO THE EXAM ON THE BIBLICAL VIEW OF SUBMISSION

1. False – Being created after Adam does not make Eve inferior to Adam any more than Adam being created after fish, birds, and animals makes him inferior to them.

2. False – Genesis 1:26-28 makes it clear that God created male and female in the image of God.

3. False – Woman was created out of man's need for her (Genesis 2:18).

4. False – God holds man – Adam – accountable for the entrance of sin into the world (Romans 5:12; 1 Corinthians 15:21-22).

5. False – Women are not responsible for the sins of men. God holds each of us accountable for our own lives. Any sin in our lives is there because of our choices, not because of someone else's choices for us.

6. False – Women are not naturally weak and evil. Nowhere does the Bible say they are to be controlled. In the home, they are to be in submission to their head, their husband. The husband is not to govern the home as a dictator but as a loving *kephale*. In the Church, women are to be under the authority of the one God has anointed and called into the position of authority, who may be a male or a female. If women are the one anointed and called to a position of leadership, they are still under higher authority, God, **as are**

all men.

7. True – Eve confessed her sin; so as far as God is concerned, there is no sin. God forgave Eve, so there is no guilt. Eve was covered by God, so there is no shame. Eve was not cursed by God; so there is no curse to bear.

> *There is therefore now no condemnation to those who are in Christ Jesus, who do not walk according to the flesh, but according to the Spirit. For the law of the Spirit of life in Christ Jesus has made me free from the law of sin and death.* (Romans 8:1-2)

8. False – Submission is imposing demands on oneself or choosing to yield to another.

9. False – The only power struggle should be that of the Holy Spirit controlling both the husband and the wife.

10. False – Submission is not a contest of human wills. Rather, God is in charge, and He makes the decisions. What He says goes.

11. False – Wives are called to submit to, not to obey, their husbands (Ephesians 5:22). Further, all Christians, including women, must obey God rather than men (Acts 5:29).

12. False – The key word is "must." True submission is when one person chooses to defer to another, even when he or she doesn't agree with the other. Submission is a choice; it is not to be demanded of or forced upon another

13. False – While Ephesians 5:22 and 1 Peter 3:1 declare that wives should be submissive to their own husbands, these verses are limited to a marriage relationship. They do not give general permission for all men to control the lives of all women.

14. False – 1 Peter 2:9 and Revelation 1:6 declare that all saints, including women, are priests. Therefore, all are

expected to function as such.

15. False – Malachi 2:16 and Ezekiel 45:9 make it clear that God opposes marital violence.

16. False – Psalm 127:3 and Matthew 18:1-6 demonstrate that God values children and that He opposes those who would harm them or who would cause them to stumble.

17. False – No Scripture supports this concept. Rather, Galatians 3:28 states that, before God, there is no male or female. If a woman is called by God, she is covered by God. She does not need to be reliant on a man to cover her.

18. False – Although Ephesians 5:22 clearly states that wives should submit to their husbands, it is preceded by Ephesians 5:21 which states that all Christians, including men, should *"be subject to one another,"* including women. Submission is a two-way street.

19. False – In Genesis 21:10-14 Abraham deferred to Sarah (with God's blessing!) when she told him to send Hagar away. In the Church, there is no gender-based hierarchy. In fact, in the Church, it is the other way around. Power and position do not begin with men placing themselves at the top. Instead, they begin with all Christians, men and women, being servants and placing themselves at the bottom.

> But Jesus called them to Himself and said, "You know that the rulers of the Gentiles lord it over them, and their great men exercise authority over them. It is not this way among you, but whoever wishes to become great among you shall be your servant." (Matthew 20:25-26)

20. True – Although the words subjection and submission are from the same Greek word *hupatasso*, their usage provides a difference in meaning. When meaning subjection, *hupatasso* is a military term meaning to rank under, to subordinate, or to make subject to. It is something done to a

person. However, when used in the middle or passive voice, *hupatasso* also means to submit or subject oneself. It is something asked of a person or something he or she chooses to do, but it can't be forced on that person.

21. True

22. True

23. True – 1 Timothy 3:1-4

24. True – An understanding of culture in the first century reveals a deeper meaning of submission here. At that time, women had few rights and were considered possessions. In the Roman Empire, what we consider a formal marriage ceremony only took place amongst those of the upper class. In contrast, the vast majority of commoners tended to "marry" in the form of *usus*. This is similar to today's common-law marriages wherein the man and woman have not been formally joined in a ceremony, yet they live together and consider themselves to be life partners. In *usus*, the wife's family retained control of her dowry, and as long as she spent three consecutive nights in her father's house each year (sometimes against her will), the father could continue to claim legal ownership of her and her property.[37]

In this context, it can be understood why Paul stressed to the new Christian community that a wife should be attached to, submitted to, or identified with her husband. She was no longer to be attached to her father. This is also why a few verses later Paul quotes Genesis 2:24: *"for this reason a man shall leave his father and mother and shall be joined to his wife, and the two shall become one flesh"* (Ephesians 5:31).

---

[37] Mirza, Sumair, and Jason Tsang. "Marriage and Customs and Roman Women," *Rome Exposed*, Classics Unveiled, 1999-2019, http://www.classicsunveiled.com/romel/html/marrcustwom.html. Accessed 10 Oct 2019.

25. True – The words for submission and *agape* love are indeed similar in meaning. Submission is not to demand rights but to give up rights. *Agape* love means to give up rights or to defer. Submission is servanthood with a good, loving attitude.

> *Love suffers long and is kind; love does not envy; love does not parade itself, is not puffed up; does not behave rudely, does not seek its own, is not provoked, thinks no evil; does not rejoice in iniquity, but rejoices in the truth; bears all things, believes all things, hopes all things, endures all things. Love never fails.* (1 Corinthians 13:4-8 NKJV)

AUTHOR'S PAGE

Susan Pryor lives in beautiful western New York State near family and friends. Early in her Christian walk, the Lord impressed the Scripture *"But we will devote ourselves to prayer and to the ministry of the word"* (Acts 6:4) into her spirit. Later, indicating one of the specific ways she was to engage in the ministry of the word, He told her to write a book. After completing the first one, several more followed, each in a small way exposing her concern that the true Church must come back to its roots in Jesus Christ and must understand that its primary reason for being is to worship God.

Other books by Susan Pryor:

Jesus is Lord

The Five-Fold Ministry: True or False

70x7: A Christian Perspective on Forgiveness

Journeys: The Parallel Journeys of the Israelites, Each Christian, and the True Church

Is Jehovah Jesus?

In The Beginning

Available through Amazon or Kindle

My deepest gratitude to my daughter, Megan Tasdeler, for her skill, patience, and persistence in editing this book and to my son-in-law, Aydin Tasdeler, for designing the cover and doing amazing technical things to publish this book and to make it a reality.